GREEK
MYTHOLOGY

© Copyright 2021 - All rights reserved.

The content contained within this book may not be reproduced, duplicated, or transmitted without direct written permission from the author or the publisher.

Under no circumstances will any blame or legal responsibility be held against the publisher, or author, for any damages, reparation, or monetary loss due to the information contained within this book, either directly or indirectly.

Legal Notice:

This book is copyright protected. It is only for personal use. You cannot amend, distribute, sell, use, quote, or paraphrase any part, or the content within this book, without the consent of the author or publisher.

Disclaimer Notice:

Please note the information contained within this document is for educational and entertainment purposes only. All effort has been executed to present accurate, up-to-date, reliable, complete information. No warranties of any kind are declared or implied. Readers acknowledge that the author is not engaged in the rendering of legal, financial, medical, or professional advice. The content within this book has been derived from various sources. Please consult a licensed professional before attempting any techniques outlined in this book.

By reading this document, the reader agrees that under no circumstances is the author responsible for any losses, direct or indirect, that are incurred as a result of the use of the information contained within this document, including, but not limited to, errors, omissions, or inaccuracies.

FREE BONUS FROM HBA: EBOOK BUNDLE

Greetings!

First of all, thank you for reading our books. As fellow passionate readers of History and Mythology, we aim to create the very best books for our readers.

Now, we invite you to join our VIP list. As a welcome gift, we offer the History & Mythology Ebook Bundle below for free. Plus, you can be the first to receive new books and exclusives! <u>Remember it's 100% free to join.</u>

Simply scan the QR code to join.

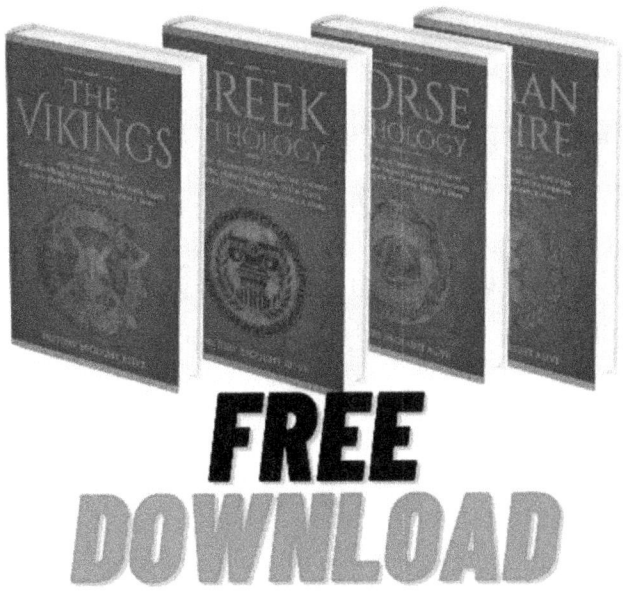

https://www.subscribepage.com/hba

Keep up to date with us on:
YouTube: History Brought Alive
Facebook: History Brought Alive
www.historybroughtalive.com

CONTENTS

INTRODUCTION 1

CHAPTER 1: WHY GREEK MYTHOLOGY IS STILL RELEVANT TODAY 8

What Were the Greek Myths? 10
What Did These Myths Teach and Do Their Teaching Still Hold Relevance? 11
Why Is Greek Mythology Still Studied? 13

CHAPTER 2: GREEK MYTHOLOGY AND ITS EVOLUTION THROUGH THE AGES 16

How Greek Mythology and Myths Influenced Ancient Greek Society 18
How Philosophers Challenged Greek Mythology and Worship of the Gods 23

CHAPTER 3: THE HISTORY OF THE WORLD ACCORDING TO GREEK MYTHOLOGY 28

The Creation of the Human Race According to Greek Mythology 36

CHAPTER 4: THE ANCIENT GREEK WORLD: WORSHIP OF THE GODS, ILLUSTRIOUS TEMPLES, AND THE MANY GREEK FESTIVALS 40

Greek Mythology as a Pagan Religion 42
Temples Built in Honor of the Greek Gods 46
Ancient Greek Festivals and Athletic Games to Honor the Gods 54

CHAPTER 5: THE GREEK PANTHEON OF MT. OLYMPUS 66

The Olympians 67

CHAPTER 6: THE MANY LARGER THAN LIFE FIGURES OF GREEK MYTHOLOGY 92

- Nymphs 93
- Centaurs 95
- Satyrs 98
- Demigods 100

CHAPTER 7: GREEK MONSTERS THAT TERRIFIED A NATION AND THREATENED THE GODS 114

- Medusa 115
- The Hydra 117
- Typhon 119
- Cerberus 122

CHAPTER 8: MYTHS THAT WITHSTOOD THE TEST OF TIME AND DEFINED A MYTHOLOGY 128

- Pandora's Jar 129
- The Myth of Icarus 131
- The Abduction of Persephone by Hades 133
- The Love Story of Eros and Psyche 136

CHAPTER 9: BATTLES AND CONQUESTS: THE TROJAN WAR AND ALEXANDER THE GREAT. 150

- The Trojan War 151
- Alexander the Great of Macedonia 159

CONCLUSION 165

REFERENCES 173

INTRODUCTION

Greek mythology is filled with fascinating myths, epic battles, awesome folklore, interesting customs, traditions, beliefs, and captivating gods and goddesses. It is sometimes seen as a daunting task to sink your teeth into something as immense and rich as Greek mythology, however, that is where History Brought Alive comes in. Throughout your captivating read, we will help you venture on a discovery to unpack all the secrets, customs, beliefs, myths, stories, and gods this fascinating ancient belief system has in store. At History Brought Alive, we are history and mythology enthusiasts. We hope you feel the same joy and excitement we do when venturing back thousands of years in the past. Join us on an adventure to discover the path of Greek mythology and learn what life was like in Ancient Greece. All the secrets of one of the most fascinating civilizations the world has ever known lie within these pages.

Throughout your read, we will not simply rehash the ancient Greek myths of the time, but rather uncover the context and background behind these myths and the Ancient Greek world. We want to make sure that you cannot only enjoy these fascinating myths but understand what they were like when they were told thousands of years ago. Through context, background, and discussion, we are able to take a peek at what life was like during ancient Greece and how life during that era was influenced by the vast array of myths. Throughout the book, we will be peeling back layers of a complex history that surround these fascinating myths to take a peek at the accurate accounts of the myths, beliefs, costumes, and traditions as they actually were.

We will uncover the creation of the universe, the gods, and the humans from the perspective of Greek mythology. We will unpack the notorious war between the gods and the Titans to understand how the gods of Greece came into power and ended up the rulers of all that the ancient Greeks knew. There are complexities to this story, family conflict, power struggles, and a lot of different agendas about who should be the ruler of the universe. Understanding the creation of the universe and the great Titan war is critical to give us a context of why Ancient Greece society operated as it did as well as the origin and importance of the Greek pantheon.

The gods played a significant role in all aspects of Ancient Greek society; thus, it is pivotal that we examine how the gods influenced the Ancient Greek world. We will unpack the ancient temples dedicated to the gods, the festivals that honor the gods, the sacrifices the Greeks made in securing favor from the gods, and how the Greeks went about their daily lives with the Greek pantheon forever weighing on their minds.

However, understanding how the Greeks worshiped the gods and how the gods played a significant role in all aspects of society is one thing, but understanding who the Greek gods and goddesses were another. We will look at all of the major gods and goddesses such as Poseidon, Hera, Ares, Hermes, Apollo, Artemis, Aphrodite, and many more iconic gods. Who they were, what they represented, the role they played in Greek society, and the myths that surrounded their legacy will all be uncovered.

Just as the gods need to be uncovered, so do the monsters, hybrids, minor deities, and demigods. We will highlight many characters that play a role in Greek mythology to get a greater understanding of the myths for all they were. Just like the gods, the other characters of Greek mythology will be highlighted in terms of who they were, what they represented, the role they played in Greek society, and the myths that surrounded their legacy.

The mythology is more than the gods and the monsters. We will discuss many myths and epic battles, highlighting all the fascinating tales that make Greek mythology an interesting belief system. Although Greek mythology is no longer followed religiously in the 21st century, there is so much we can learn from the ancient religion. The epic tales and myths are filled with lessons, philosophies, cautionary warning signs, and golden nuggets about life. It is still an important academic topic that merits study and understanding to this day.

The legends, myths, and stories are all here just waiting to be read. Everything you need to know about the Ancient Greeks and the Greek pantheon is neatly wrapped up in one single read. All that is left to do is for you to uncover the secrets of the Ancient Greek world. Discover what life was like thousands of years ago in the Mediterranean and what governed these people's customs, traditions, and beliefs.

CHAPTER 1
WHY GREEK MYTHOLOGY IS STILL RELEVANT TODAY

There is a reason why mythological beliefs are still studied to this day. These myths were not just stories and epic tales but were a guiding system of humanity for hundreds of years that provided lessons, morals, hope, and comfort, and played a crucial role in developing how we shaped modern thinking.

If there is one subject of history that is still taught today and has stood the test of time, it is Greek mythology. Greek mythology is not just taught as a part of the literature curriculum in high school but also forms part of most history lessons to uncover the hidden secrets of humanity's past.

Many people may be wondering how mythology as ancient as Greek mythology still lingers in the world's collective mind. Many may view the ancient Greek myths as nothing more than stories that were told thousands of years ago and believe they hold no value in modern society. However, if you stop and look at the vast amount of influence Greek mythology has had on popular culture such as in countless movies, TV shows, and books it quickly becomes clear that Greek mythology still fascinates the modern world.

Throughout this chapter, we will highlight why the Greek myths have withstood the test of time, still remain relevant, and will remain relevant for centuries to come.

What Were the Greek Myths?

To many people the ancient Greek myths will simply only be viewed as epic tales of the Greek pantheon gallivanting around the earth, going on crazy adventures, and achieving all sorts of supernatural feats. This is true, but only on the surface. If you only view these tales with tunnel vision, then you will only believe them to be ancient fairytales. However, if you look beyond the bloody tales, epic battles, and the supernatural, you will see that these myths are more than simple legends. A deeper look will help you uncover the lessons, morals, philosophies, and even warnings that these myths taught the ancient Greek world and quite honestly still teaches modern civilization to this day.

Take note that very few of these stories have happy endings, which is something the world has become very accustomed to today. There are often no happy endings in Greek mythology as they were not stories that were written for the purpose of entertainment. Instead, they were stories to teach, understand the world, and a model for ancient Greeks to ensure their actions were in line with.

These stories, or myths, were not designed to tell a story for the sake of telling a story, but, instead, played a crucial role in ancient Greek society to impart knowledge from generation to generation. The stories open windows for us to see into the past and their lessons are still true today. It allows us to catch a glimpse of what the lives of the ancient Greek populace were like back then.

What Did These Myths Teach and Do Their Teaching Still Hold Relevance?

These myths were passed down by the ancient Greek populace from generation to generation. They were told with the purpose to help Greeks realize the difference between what is right and what is wrong. In an era where Greek mythology was at its pinnacle, law and order were not, and thus the differentiation between what is right and wrong was critical. Even today the understanding of what is right and what is wrong is an integral cog in a functional society.

The myths also taught the Greeks the importance of humility, selflessness, caring for those you love, and never thinking of themselves as being immortal as they would be punished for such foolishness. It taught the Greeks to always remain pure of heart and resist the urges of temptation and corruption, as Zeus would punish the corrupt and disobedient with great wrath. All of these teachings are still very prevalent in the modern world.

The myths also told the Greeks about the tales of heroes and how true greatness would be achieved by those who dared and lived life courageously. However, these same tales showed the flaws of these very same heroes, signifying that everyone has flaws and nobody is perfect, no matter how they may seem. These lessons remain true to this day.

Any person from the 21st century who hears or reads about a Greek myth is almost guaranteed to see the relevance of some of the lessons these ancient stories taught humanity. Anybody, no matter who they are, who picks up a book on Greek myths is likely to learn a thing or two other than simply being entertained.

Why Is Greek Mythology Still Studied?

The truth is reading and hearing about Greek mythology and the ancient myths is one thing, however, studying the matter is another. Thus, the question that many may have been why are these mythological beliefs still being studied in the 21st century? The answer is to learn. Plainly put and said, we still study Greek mythology in the 21st century as we want to know how the Ancient Greeks lived. Studying to understand how the Ancient Greeks lived is no different than an anthropologist studying how the Khoi-san people of South Africa live. We study ancient cultures not only to understand the culture but to learn from them too.

After all, after studying a culture as progressive as the ancient Greeks and breaking

down how they lived and what they believed in, you really can't help but learn a thing or two. These myths are time capsules. They show the modern human how humanity's concept of the world compares to their own. It allows 21st-century humans to glance at the past, see what the ancient Greeks considered important, how their civilization operated, what their moral compass looked like, and how they viewed the world with extremely limited scientific explanations they had access to. What's more, studying ancient Greek myths has helped us understand classic literature. Greek mythology has also contributed to and influenced many box office hits, TV shows, modern literature, comics, and more.

It has been said by experts that by studying or even simply reading Greek mythology, people tend to have more control of their actions and utilize more rational thinking before they act due to the teachings of the myths (Smith, 2020). This is an interesting claim as many of the Greek myths communicate tales about how humanity's stupidity, follies, and hubris constantly land humankind in danger. Perhaps being versed in the myths makes you second guess your actions' consequences. What is ironic is that people to this day still tend to be guided by foolishness, give in to temptation, make selfish or stupid decisions, and possess excessive pride despite the warnings and teachings of Greek mythology. It is quite humorous to witness just how accurately the ancient Greek myths still capture the essence of human behavior and is relevant to how 21st-century human behaves.

CHAPTER 2
GREEK MYTHOLOGY AND ITS EVOLUTION THROUGH THE AGES

Greek mythology, as with many other cultures and beliefs at the time, was used as an instrument to help humans understand the world and environment on a grander scale. This greater understanding that Greek mythology bestowed upon ancient inhabitants of Greece provided insight regarding how humankind lived, the natural phenomenon the world experienced, as well as the passing of time as day turned into night and days, turned into weeks, months and years.

What we now call mythology was a collection of stories, beliefs, and traditions designed to help the citizens of Greece lead happy, fulfilled lives. They sought to explain the origins of the gods, the origins of man, and where the deceased souls depart after death. Myths were also used as a form of documentation to re-tell historical events to the greater public so that the citizens of ancient Greece could remain and sustain contact with their ancestors, the wars Greece fought, and the lands that the Greeks explored.

How Greek Mythology and Myths Influenced Ancient Greek Society

In modern society, the term "myth" is largely associated with negative connotations and is often believed to be a rumor or story that lacks sufficient authenticity or reliability to be considered factual. However, when Greek mythology was flourishing from 3000 B.C.E. to 1100 B.C.E., myths were whole-heartedly believed by many. However, as with everything, especially with a religious or non-written source, there would always be those who believed and those who discounted the authenticity of the source.

The myths were largely used for educational and religious purposes to help mankind get a greater grasp of the world around them. However, it is important to realize that myths played a large part in influencing entertainment at the time in Ancient Greece. Much of what we know today about Ancient Greece and Greek mythology is due to the many forms of artistic representations of the myths themselves. It is evident that the myths of ancient Greece were incredibly popular and familiar to a wide section of Greek society due to the common representation of the myths through art, such as paintings, sculptures, and pottery.

Literacy was not common in ancient Greece, thus myths were relayed orally amongst Greek citizens. Famous Greek bards, such as Minoan and Mycenaean, from the 18th Century B.C.E., and onwards, were often found passing the myths of Greek mythology through song. Due to the fact that the myths of Greek mythology were often passed on orally, there was a large possibility that, with each re-telling of the myths, they would be embellished and improved upon. The myths themselves would evolve as they were passed on through the ages largely due to word of mouth. The evolution of the myths could largely boil down to the stories being told in such a way to improve an audience's interest, relating the story to the era they were being told in, and incorporating local events and prejudices into the myths.

It is also likely that the re-telling of myths in the world of art and storytelling in Ancient Greece followed a particular set of rules of presentation. This is because a knowledgeable audience may not be as willing to accept an ad hoc adaptation of the myths they were familiar with. However, over centuries of the citizens of Ancient Greece having increased contact with other city-states and trading with each other, it is hard to imagine that the myths and local stories did not get muddled up with one another thus leading to myths with several diverse origins.

The next major development at the time was around the 8th century B.C.E., when the presentation of myths took place in the form of poems, with epic poems being written by brilliant poets such as Homer and Hesiod in Ionia.

This was revolutionary because this was the first time the myths had been presented in written form as literacy levels in Greece began to rise. Homer's epic poem Iliad presents the final stages of the Trojan War. The Trojan War is incredibly significant to the Ancient Greeks as it is an amalgamation of various conflicts between the Greeks and many of their neighboring Eastern borders. The Trojan War took place between 1800B.C.E. and 1200B.C.E. during the late stages of the Bronze Age. In Odyssey, written by Homer, the poem recounts the protracted voyage home of the Greek hero Odysseus following his fierce battle in the Trojan War.

Other significant poems at the time were written by Hesiod and included Theogony as well as Works and Days. In the poem of Theogony, Hesiod provides the world with a genealogy of the Greek gods for the very first time in written form. Hesiod's Works and Days poem retells the story of the creation of man from a Greek mythological perspective. What is incredibly interesting about these poems is that the gods themselves are generally described with typically human feelings and faults, but in the end, heroes are created and born.

After poetry had been introduced as a form of representation of the gods and myths, the next introduction to the retelling and documentation of Greek mythology came in the form of pottery from around the 8th century B.C.E. onwards. Ancient Greece often utilized pottery as an art form to portray the gods and myths with a myriad of mythical scenes frozen in time as they were decorated on ceramics of all shapes and sizes.  The pottery that came out of Ancient Greece at the time was absolutely breathtaking. These beautifully crafted pots spread the myths through art to a wider audience and relayed the stories of the gods throughout Ancient Greece thus the myths evolved once again through a new medium.

Throughout the centuries, the myths continued to be popular and had a major influence on society. As a result of the surging popularity and influence, many major temples were built in honor of these stories and legends. These included the Parthenon in Athens, the Temple of Zeus in Olympia, and the Temple of Apollo in Delphi. However, there were many more examples of beautiful temples built in the name of the gods. These grand architectural marvels of the world were decorated with larger-than-life sculptures to represent and celebrate the legendary scenes of Greek mythology and the myths that had been passed down for centuries.

In the 5th century B.C.E., the myths were represented in a new format. The myths were now beginning to be told in the theater in the form of plays. The theatre provided an opportunity for the myths to be presented in a theatrical display and were largely told by three major tragedians: Aeschylus, Sophocles, and Euripides.

Just before the introduction of the theater, the myths started to see skepticism about their authenticity in the 6th century B.C.E. The first rejections and skepticism of the myths had been documented in writing and thus began the era of pre-Socratic philosophers. These philosophers wanted to gain a greater scientific explanation for natural phenomena and events. Finally, in the 5th century B.C.E., the pioneers of modern history, Herodotus and Thucydides, began to document phenomena to a greater degree of accuracy (as accurate as they possibly could at the time) and bestowed it upon themselves to take a less subjective view of phenomena and events. Due to this shift in thinking, and a new approach to understanding the natural world with a greater scientific approach, the subject of history was born.

How Philosophers Challenged Greek Mythology and Worship of the Gods

In Ancient Greece the gods were all-powerful and they all admired beings of the universe. However, during the 6th century B.C.E., a new wave of thinking took place, and the age of Greek philosophy was born. The philosophers, unlike the majority of the Greek populace at the time, looked to challenge the beliefs of the Greek pantheon and wanted to view the world from a more scientific perspective. This movement began during the period of the Ionian philosophers, particularly due to the work of one of the founding fathers of philosophy, Anaximander. Anaximander was the first scholar to have made a map of the inhabited world and developed a theory of the creation of the world without the influence of the Greek pantheon. Anaximander came up with a theory of the origin of the world known as the concept of the Apeiron.

Anaximander explains this theory as "the first principle and element of existing things was boundless . . . he has creation take place not as a result of any of the elements undergoing qualitative change, but as a result of the opposites being separated off by the means of motion, which is eternal," (Decibelboy, 2012).

Anaximander's views of the creation of the world through the concept of Apeiron is the first time that somebody had taken the perspective of the creation of the world as, if not scientific, at least a perspective that is non-mythic. However, having said this Anaximander's attempts to explain the realities of the world the Ancient Greeks were living in were still tied within a mythic context as it seemed he still considered the Aperion to be a result of divine intervention. However, what is important was that it completely ignored the influence of the Greek pantheon.

Anaximander's views birthed a new revolution and led to the inspiration of countless philosophers. Another great philosopher around the same time as Anaximander was Xenophanes. He too had his own theory of the universe outside of the influence of the Greek gods. Xenophanes' ideas were strongly linked to a reason. He was known to challenge the ideas of the anthropomorphic gods.

However, at the pinnacle of the use of reason, scientific perspective, and logic to challenge the ancient Greek myths was the legendary philosopher, Socrates. Socrates himself did not write a single word, however, his teachings were used extensively by the Greek philosopher Plato. Thanks to Plato's work, we can learn from Socrates' beliefs through the dialogues Plato had documented. Through this documentation, we are able to learn about how Socrates challenged the gods and are left to see how many holes in the myths of Greek mythology have been prodded upon through arguments of science, reason, and logic.

However, Socrates' story does not end well, as the ruling classes of ancient Greece took a dislike to the teachings of Socrates and would sentence the philosopher to his death. This is an incredibly important event in the evolution of Greek society and the progression of classical mythology. Before the philosophers, the myths of the ancient Greek world were used as a means to understand and explore the realities of the world. However, at this point in history, it seems it was the first time that the myths' power as tools of explanation had been credibly challenged. These challenges to the ancient myths represented a desire among the Greek populace to escape from what they had been brought up to believe and move towards a more logical explanation of the realities of the world.

The ruling bodies of the ancient Greek world were not fond of this idea and realized that if this

was left unpunished, problems would occur from Socrates' new logical thinking. The ruling bodies believed that if Socrates was allowed to continue expressing his views it would change their society and everything in it which the ruling classes would not accept. Instead, they would act, by labeling all philosophers as criminals, to ensure that the myths stay intact to shield the majority of the Greek populace from this new form of thinking. Thus, this marked the age where there was a divide in belief between those who believed in the gods and those who desired to seek a more logical and scientific explanation of the world.

CHAPTER 3
THE HISTORY OF THE WORLD ACCORDING TO GREEK MYTHOLOGY

In Ancient Greece, the Greek populace created myths that helped them understand and explain the world around them and help them to better understand the human condition. In Greek Mythology, the world began with one entity known as Chaos, the first goddess of the known world according to the Greeks. Chaos was believed to be a gaping hole of emptiness that gave birth to the world as we know it. Out of Chaos's dark and empty formless void sprang forth three more deities known as Gaea, the goddess of the Earth, Tartarus, the dark abyss of the Underworld, and Eros, the god of love. When Eros was born, the two goddesses, Chaos and Gaea, were able to procreate and bring life into the universe and thus the known Universe began to take shape.

The Children of Chaos and Gaea

The great poet, Hesiod, wrote an epic poem during the 8th century B.C.E. about the creation of the world, titled Theogony. According to Hesiod's poem, three crucial elements played a role in the creation of the world. These elements included Chaos, Gaea, and Eros. In the poem of Theogony, it is stated that Chaos slept with Eros and gave birth to Erebus, the god of darkness, and Nyx, the goddess of the night. Chaos's children Erebus and Nyx formed a romantic union and gave birth to Aether, who was the bright upper air of the world, and Hemera, who brought the daytime. Nyx would go on to have twelve more children, each representing other parts of nature and life. Nyx's twelve children included the hateful Moros (fate), Hypnos (sleep), Momos (blame), Philotes (sexual pleasure), Apate (Deceit), Eris (Strife), Oizus (pain), Nemesis (Revenge), Ker (Doom), Oneiroi (Dreams and Nightmares), Geras (Old Age), Thanatos (Death), and Hesperides (the daughter of the evening).

While Chaos and Nyx had their own children, Gaea gave birth to Uranus (who created the story sky) and Oceanus (who created the oceans). Uranus was appointed as Gaea's protector, and over the years the two of them became lovers and were the first gods to rule over the world as we know it. Uranus and Gaea had eighteen children. Twelve of these children would be born as Titans, three of these children were born as Cyclopes, and three were known as Hecatoncheires (monstrous giants with 50 heads and 100 arms).

The Tyrant Rule of Uranus

However, the union between Gaea and Uranus was not a peaceful one. Uranus was a cruel husband, but an even crueler father. Uranus was threatened by his children's divine powers and was afraid that one day his children would rise up and overthrow him to claim the throne of ruler of the world. In an attempt to ensure his children would never rise above him, Uranus made sure that none of his children were to see the light of day again and imprisoned them in the hidden place of the Earth—Gaea's womb.

At first, Gaea agreed to this unjust punishment as a result of being heavily manipulated by her husband. However, as the years passed, Gaea could not sit idle any longer. Gaea devised a plan to rid her children of their abusive father's clutches, in doing so Gaea handed over a sickle to her youngest son, the Titan Cronus. After giving her son the sickle, Gaea arranged a meeting between Cronus and Uranus. Cronus used the sickle to cut off Uranus' genitals. The seed of Uranus fell into the ocean, creating Aphrodite, the goddess of beauty. The blood that fell from Uranus's severed testicles created the Fates, the

Giants, and the Meliad nymphs.

The Titan Ruler Cronus

Uranus's fears turned into reality and his son overthrew him to take the throne. As the new ruler, he imprisoned his Cyclopes and Hecatonchires siblings in the prison of Tartarus (the Underworld), guarded by a fierce dragon. Cronus married his Titan sister, Rhea, and freed all of his siblings. Once all of Cronus's siblings were freed from their earthly prisons, Cronos shared his kingdom with them. All of Cronus's brothers and sisters were given duties and responsibilities they needed to fulfill. His brother, Oceanus, was given the responsibility to rule over all the oceans, seas, and rivers. Another of Cronus's brothers, Hyperion, was responsible for the sun and the stars.

Cronus and Rhea had five children of their own. According to Greek mythology experts, it is believed that Cronus's parents, Gaea and Uranus, prophesied that Cronus would also be overthrown by one of his sons, just as his father was. Haunted with fear, history repeated itself and Cronus imprisoned his children.

Cronus eventually decided that the best way to deal with this problem was to swallow all his children the moment they were born. Like Gaea, Rhea was horrified and would not stand for the mistreatment of her children and devised a plan to save her children. Rhea tricked Cronus by wrapping a stone in infant clothing and presenting it to Cronus as the sixth child. Cronus fell for the deceit and swallowed the stone whole thinking he had devoured his newborn son.

Rhea managed to hide Zeus from Cronus and left the newborn god on the island of Crete, where he was raised by the Nymphs of Mount Dikte. When Zeus was growing up, the Kouretes (Creatures who worshiped the goddess Cybele with drumming and dancing) would clash their shields together and dance to cover up the sound of Zeus crying. Years passed and Zeus entered manhood and gained unparalleled strength.

The Return of Zeus

Zeus had grown into an extremely handsome and powerful adult. The time had come to return to his homeland to defeat his father and free his siblings from his clutches. Zeus left Crete and unbeknownst to him asked his future wife, the Titan Metis, the god of wisdom, for advice on how to defeat his tyrant father. Metis replied with a seamless plan. She told Zeus to prepare a poisonous drink that was indistinguishable from Cronus's favorite wine. This drink would be designed to make Cronus vomit and slowly poison him. Zeus was delighted with this plan and executed it to perfection. Zeus disguised himself as one of the Kingdom's cupbearers and successfully slipped Metis's drink into Cronus's glass of wine.

The plan worked like a charm and Cronus began vomiting uncontrollably. As Cronus began to vomit, each one of Zeus's five siblings was expelled from their tyrant father's stomach. Zeus was united for the first time with his siblings Hestia, Demeter, Hera, Hades, and Poseidon. Zeus's siblings were overwhelmed with gratitude and immediately recognized Zeus as their leader who would bring down Cronus's tyrannical rule.

The Final Hurdle of the Gods Versus the TItans

Although Zeus had managed to free his siblings from his father's imprisonment, Cronus was still in command and was yet to be defeated. However, thanks to Zeus, the Titan ruler was greatly weakened. As it stood, Cronus was too old to protect himself from the onslaught of his progeny, so he enlisted the help of his most faithful Titan soldiers and followers. The war between the Titans and the Olympians lasted for an entire decade and is remembered by generations as the Titanomachy. Cronus enlisted Atlas as the Titan's leader in arms and he led the Titan army to many victories. In fact, for a long stage of the war, it seemed that the Olympians would lose and all of Zeus's efforts would be for nothing. However, Zeus was approached by Gaea who advised him to visit Tartarus and release the imprisoned Cyclopes and Hecatoncheires. Zeus listened and freed the prisoners and in gratitude the Cyclopes gifted Zeus with his legendary thunderbolt. The Cyclopes also provided Poseidon with his trident and gifted Hades with the helmet of invisibility. With these new weapons and equipment, the tables had turned and the Olympians were well on their way to victory.

Greek mythology is filled with stories of cunning succeeding over brute strength. The final battle between the Titans and the Olympians was no different. The victory for the Olympians was the result of a cunning, little trick, credited to the Titan Prometheus. Armed with boulders, the one-hundred-armed Hecatoncheires set an ambush for the Titans. Zeus retreated his army to draw the Titans into the Hecatoncheires trap, in which the Titans would be met with a storm of boulders plummeting to the ground from the sky. The Titans fell for the trap. Hundreds of boulders rained down on the Titan troops with such fury that the Titan army thought that the entire mountain range was falling down upon them. The Titans retreated and surrendered. After ten long and bloody years of war, the Olympians were awarded victory and Zeus could finally consider himself the king of the Universe. Zeus immediately exiled all the Titans who fought against him to the depths of Tartarus, however, he made an exception for one. He punished Atlas to an even greater degree as Atlas was sentenced to hold the universe on his shoulders for the rest of eternity.

The Creation of the Human Race According to Greek Mythology

According to the myths, the Olympian Gods thought it would be interesting to create beings in their own image, but as mortals without divine powers, to inhabit the earth. When the mortals were created, Zeus ordered Prometheus and Epitameus, the sons of the Titan Iapetus, to bestow various gifts among the mortals. Zeus ordered these gifts to be given to the mortals as he hoped that the human race would evolve into interesting creatures that would act as a source of amusement for the gods.

Thus, Prometheus and Epitamus began to divide these gifts among themselves and started to give them to the new inhabitants of Earth. It was decided between the two brothers that Prometheus would hand out the first gifts. Prometheus handed out the gifts to the animals first. He handed some animals beauty, some animals were given strength, others were given agility, and the rest were given speed. However, Prometheus left the mortal humans defenseless and did not give them any natural weapons. Prometheus loved mankind and realized the error of his ways, and to make up for his error, he promptly distributed his own gifts to mankind in the form of superior intellect and reasoning. He stole the gift of reason from the goddess Athena and bestowed it upon man. Prometheus then stole fire from the gates of Hephaestus to make sure that the humans could keep themselves warm and cook. Due to Prometheus taking a liking to mankind, he shared all the knowledge he had with them and became the protector of the human race.

However, Prometheus did not consult Zeus. Zeus was furious. Until that point, a fire had been reserved for the use of the gods and Zeus did not want the mortals to resemble the gods. Due to Prometheus's negligence, he was heavily punished. Prometheus was chained up for thirty years on the peak of the Caucasus, hovering over the edge of the world. Every day, an eagle would feast on his liver, only for it to grow back the next day. However, after thirty years the seemingly never-ending nightmare came to an end. Herakles (Hercules) relieved Prometheus from his punishment and he was allowed to return back to the land of the gods.

CHAPTER 4
THE ANCIENT GREEK WORLD: WORSHIP OF THE GODS, ILLUSTRIOUS TEMPLES, AND THE MANY GREEK FESTIVALS

In ancient Greece, there were very specific customs, cultures, worship practices, and traditions that were held in high regard by the overwhelming populace of the time. The Ancient Greeks were famous for demonstrating the utmost admiration for the gods by instilling several rituals and celebrations to honor and appease the gods that they both loved and feared at the same time. They also practiced and instilled these customs as a way to ensure harmony with the gods. Thus, it is fair to say that Ancient Greek culture was a product that was molded by appeasing their many gods. There are various examples of how the Greeks showed their admiration and prayers to the god such as sacrifices, temples, festivals, and even games that were formed to honor the gods.

Greek Mythology as a Pagan Religion

The religion which the Greeks practiced can often be seen as a heavy influence over other Pagan religions which also believed in and worshiped several gods instead of simply one divine being. This can be seen in Roman mythology, Egyptian mythology, Norse mythology, and many other polytheistic religions. This is because many of these Pagan cultures and beliefs would overlap with one another due to the various different cultures coming in contact with one another through trade and travel. The citizens of different regions would converse with one another and trade stories about their beliefs and their gods, thus mythological aspects from various forms of mythology were borrowed and adapted. This is especially evident with the Greeks and the Romans who shared a very similar belief system. Both the Greek and Roman myths and tales shared strikingly similar aspects throughout their respective ancient religions.

Greek mythology is classified as a Pagan religion as it was polytheistic. This means the Ancient Greeks worshipped many gods and goddesses, each one representing a piece of the human condition, and were often used as a means to help understand the world. The ancient Greeks believed that by worshipping multiple gods, they were granted an opportunity of a great sense of freedom as they could relate to the gods that they felt most resonated with them. This sense of freedom that Greek mythology awarded the populace of Greece, and many other Pagan religions was an aspect that the followers of the mythology treasured.

During the era when Ancient Greece reigned supreme, between 700 B.C.E. and 480 B.C.E., they were well known for their intellectual distinction from other nations of the world at the time and their means of worship played a significant role in that. What was so interesting about the Ancient Greek world was that although they believed in Greek mythology their perception and views on their ancient religion were quite drastically different depending on the region the Greeks lived in. In Greek society, each city-state, also known as polis, was believed to have a specific god or gods protecting and guiding the residents of that region. Each polis had its own set of gods watching over them meant that the belief of common gods in a region would help unify the residents that populated it. What is evident in Ancient Greece was the idea that the Greek populace at the time was yearning for a distinct unity and order in the universe that they inhabited. The Greek citizens took a lot of comfort knowing that the universe was always balanced thanks to the gods they believed in.

It may seem rather contradictory that the Greeks yearned for organization and order while still worshiping multiple gods, as the connotations of multiple gods would generally be assumed to create confusion and disorder. However, to the Ancient Greeks, the gods were not only gods but symbols and representations. Each god would uphold a distinct role in the universe and represent a different part of life thus as a unit they would be known to be the organizing body of the universe if each god was pleased and honored.

Beyond the gods being representations of the human condition, they would also be used as a means to help justify any phenomenon that could not be understood. For example, the Ancient Greeks believed that when thunder and lightning fell from the sky it was because Zeus the god of skies (particularly lightning) was punishing humans as he was irate with them. The Greeks would believe that they had angered Zeus due to some wrong doing they must have committed or perhaps their worship of the god of thunder was inadequate. However, to ensure that the gods were happy and appeased with humans, the Greeks would participate in activities such as prayer, sacrifice, building temples, and engaging in festivals in the name of their gods.

There was even evidence of the institutionalization of the gods in the form of a hierarchy. The main gods of the Greek pantheon would include the 12 gods of Olympus and below them would be smaller and more minor deities, thus creating the reign of the Olympian gods and forming the Olympian religion. However, as said early not all gods were worshiped equally, and depending on the region or polis that Greeks lived in would play a role in which gods were considered more desirable than others.

The Ancient Greeks, like many other pagan or polytheistic beliefs, viewed their gods as having flaws. The Greek pantheon was not "flawless"; they had their faults and the Greeks recognized them. This is quite contrasting to many other monotheistic belief systems such as Christianity or Judaism which regard their respective God as being all-powerful, all-forgiving, and without flaws. The Greek pantheon was portrayed as human-like figures who would make mistakes and felt human emotions, often succumbing to these emotions at times. The Greek pantheon was known to experience pain, envy, anguish, greed, jealousy, and even greed. These emotions are ever-present in the myths of the Greek pantheon and more often than not the Greek gods and goddesses' emotions that they experienced would dictate their actions.

What separates greek mythology even more from Christianity was that the Ancient Greek religion was ritual-based and was a religion with flexible belief systems without traditional clergymen. Above that, Greek mythology did not institute any real sacred texts or enforce a definitive moral code that the Greek populace needed to abide by. Like many other Pagan religions, the tales and worship of the gods were primarily oral and thus documentation is scarce. This was because religion and culture heavily relied on spoken stories, myths, and tales that survived through the oral tradition of Ancient Greece. Ancient Greek culture was heavily reliant on oral forms of communication as most of the Greek populace was illiterate and thus were unable to accurately document their lives, beliefs, myths, and legends in written form for many years.

Temples Built in Honor of the Greek Gods

In Ancient Greece, many temples were built and acted as a center of worship for the Ancient Greeks to honor and appease the gods. These temples were believed to be the home of gods and

goddesses. In each temple, there were servants who would serve the house of the gods and worship their honor through prayer and sacrificial offerings. The sacrifices made in the temples needed to be conducted by higher-ups, as no ordinary man nor woman could enter the temple, as it was forbidden in Ancient Greek customs. Instead, ordinary men and women would have to worship the gods from outside the temples of the gods or more often than not in their own homes. However, if they were to workshop the gods by the temple they would generally have to worship the gods around the Temenos, which was a natural feature that generally surrounded the temple. Temenos was generally a creek or a cave around which the temple of the gods would be built around. Within the Temenos, Ancient Greeks would generally hold festivals as this was an ideal opportunity to worship and celebrate the gods in large numbers of people. Festivals were an opportunity for the Greek populace to show their undying appreciation and admiration for the gods of the Ancient Greek world.

It was evident that temples were a significant aspect of Ancient Greece and were a significant factor that shaped the lives and customs of all Greek people at the time. The Greeks believed that if they provided sacrifices to the gods and if they showed consistent admiration and devotion through prayer that the gods would favor them and provide them with a great fortune in life, safe passage, and even assist them in war. To many Greeks, showing respect to their gods was what they believed their life purpose to be, and temples provided a tangible platform to achieve their desired purpose in life.

Temple of Olympian Zeus in Ancient Athens, Greece

Today only fragments of the illustrious Temple of Zeus in Athens still remain as it is believed most of the temple was destroyed as a result of the earthquakes of AD 522 and 511. Although only a few columns remain of the grand temple of the god of the lightning, it does not take much imagination to realize just how enormous the temple was. The temple of Olympian Zeus was located in Athens and was known as the Olympian, it was a 15-acre building that was just Southeast of the Acropolis. However, in ancient times, Zeus's temple would be located in a city known as Olympia. In Ancient Greece, the city of Olympia was the center of worship for Zeus, the king of the Olympian gods, and was the home of the cult of Zeus. In Olympia, there were many smaller temples, monuments, altars, theaters, bathhouses, and beautiful statues that were all built in honor of the mighty Zeus. The Temple of Olympian Zeus was also the location where the original Olympic games would be held every four years to honor Zeus and the other Greek pantheon.

The construction of the Temple of Olympian Zeus in Ancient Athens was believed to have started around the 6th century B.C.E. This construction was done during the time Athens was ruled by Athenian tyrants. These tyrants envisaged a temple so large and so grand that it would be known throughout the ancient world. Although the construction of Zeus's temple in Athens was started by the Athenian tyrants, the temple was not completely finished under their rule. The temple in honor of the King of Olympians was completed in the 2nd century B.C.E. Zeus' temple was completed under the rule of the Roman Emperor, Hadrian, and took an astonishing 638 years in total. The end result was a marvelous temple, which was one of, if not the most, impressive temples in all the known ancient world—just how the tyrant Athenian rulers envisioned it to be. Zeus's temple in Ancient Greece stood at an enormous height of precisely 68 feet. The temple was also 95 feet wide and 235 feet long. The size of Zeus's temple was almost unimaginable and was one of the seven wonders of the ancient world.

Temple of Poseidon at Sounion in Athens, Greece

Poseidon was one of the most celebrated gods of the known Greek world and was known to be the god of the ocean. Poseidon was one of Zeus's brothers, thus it is no surprise the Greeks constructed an incredibly beautiful and lavish temple to honor him. The illustrious temple in honor of Poseidon was built on the Greek cape of Sounion, located on the coastline of Athens. This was a very fitting location for a temple honoring the god of the Ocean. This beautiful temple's construction was estimated to take place between the years 444 and 440 B.C.E. The temple was built almost entirely from marble that was sourced from the valley of Agrilesa, about two and a half miles (four kilometers) north of the beautiful cape of Sounion. It is believed that the architect was Ictinus, the same architect who erected the Temple of Hephaestus located in Athens in the Ancient Agora and built the Temple of Poseidon.

Ictinus built Poseidon's temple with 16 columns as he knew that this would help it stand the test of time and would withstand the environmental damage. However, today the temple is only a remnant of its former design. Another clever addition to Poseidon's temple that Ictinus added was to make the Doric columns more slender at the top so that it would create the impression that the temple was actually taller than it was.

As Poseidon was the god of the ocean, it was only logical that a god considered so powerful and significant would be highly revered and worshiped in a country that is accompanied by over 8,390 miles (13,500 kilometers) of coastline. In Ancient Greece, it was a general belief among the populace, especially sailors, that Poseidon would bring upon treacherous storms as a sign of his wrath when he was displeased with humans. For this reason, Poseidon's temple located at the Sounion Cape was a highly sacred location. It was a temple where many sailors, and the general population, would come to offer sacrifices and gifts in order to appease Poseidon to entice him to provide good fortune for the Greek populace and safe travel upon the oceans.

Temple of Hera in Samos

The goddess Hera, goddess of fertility, marriage, woman, and family was believed to have four major temples built in her honor, however, the temple dedicated to Hera in Samos is considered the marvel of them all. Hera was the main deity of Samos, and it was believed that Samos was in fact the birthplace of the great goddess. For this reason, the Temple of Hera was considered the sanctuary of ancient Samos and was one of the most significant sanctuaries in all of the known ancient world.

The temple is located on the southeast coast of Greece and is approximately four miles (six kilometers) away from the Ancient Island Samos which is today known as Pythagorion, however, the temple was connected to Samos by a road which was known as the "holy road."

The temple began to be constructed around about 540 B.C.E. which was during the rule of the tyranny of Polycrates (538 to 522 B.C.E.). The architects credited for the grand design of Hera's temple were Theodorus and Telecles. The temple was enormous, to say the least, and was almost immeasurable for the time. However, it is believed that the temple in all its glory was 368 feet (112.2

meters) long, 181 feet (55.16 meters) wide, and 70.5 feet (21.5 meters) high. It was a goliath. Hera's grand temple had 155 pillars to hold up the enormous structure in which historians have managed to distinguish that four different types and sizes of pillars were used in the construction of the goddesses' temple. However, due to the temple's age and the harshness of the environment, only one pillar at half the original height remains. Greeks from all regions would come to offer sacrifices, and gifts in honor of the goddess of love and marriage to show their gratitude and attempt to gain good fortune with the goddess.

The location of Hera's temple is also significant as not only is the temple they believed location of the goddess' birth but is also supposedly where Hera and Zeus were married. On top of that, according to Greek mythology, humans found a wooden statue of Hera in this very location, however, it was believed that the wooden statue was not carved by human hands. As a result of this discovery, the populace of Samos was convinced that the presence of the deity was present in these lands. Thus, it was decided that the creation of a temple to represent the sanctuary in honor of the goddess Hera was imperative. This decision was made despite the fact that they knew the area in which the temple would be constructed was not conducive due to the unstable terrain due to the erosion caused by the river Imravos.

Ancient Greek Festivals and Athletic Games to Honor the Gods

In Ancient Greece, festivals and athletic games were a crucial component of the ancient religious practices of the Greeks to honor, respect, and show admiration towards their gods. The purposes of the festivals all differed and played different roles in terms of worship, however, what was common among all the festivals was a common desire to maintain a good relationship with the gods and praise them to bestow great fortune amongst the Greek populace. Festivals were plentiful in Ancient Greece, particularly in Athens, the Greeks would set aside approximately 60 days a year to be dedicated in honor and worship of the Greek pantheon. These festivals and athletic games were forever recurring and were major religious events that would either be practiced annually every two years or every four years depending on the nature of the festival.

The festivals were strategically organized by

the Greeks so that at least one of the festivals or athletic games would fall each year, in truth many festivals were held every year. The oldest and most prominent festival of athletic games was known as the Olympic games which were held in honor of Zeus and were practiced at his temple in Olympia every four years. The Olympic games are still held to this day, however, the nature of the event has evolved significantly and is no longer exclusive to just the Greek populace.

Olympia was one of the Greeks' oldest religious centers and the worship hub of the king of the Olympians, Zeus. So, it was logical that their most esteemed festival would be held in the region of the country where Zeus was worshipped the most extensively. The games would always recur at the same site—the Temple of Olympian Zeus. Other festivals other than the Olympic games were also hosted on a major religious site, such as a temple dedicated to the god or goddesses. For all the festivals and games, there would be messengers who would announce the dates of when the festivals would commence so that everybody across the land could come and partake in the celebrations and worship of the gods.

The Olympic Games

The first-ever Olympic games were held in 776 B.C.E., and unlike its modern iteration of the event, there was only one competition—the foot race. There are two myths that the foot race is representative. The first myth is that the foot race symbolizes how the guardian nymphs of an infant Zeus hosted the first-ever foot race, and the other myth is that the foot race hosted by the first-ever Olympic games symbolizes Zeus's victory over his father Cronus in his race to control the entire world.

The footrace that commenced at the first Olympic games was 600 feet long and was the only event that would take place for the first 13 iterations of the event. However, over time the Greeks decided that it was time for the games to evolve and added the pentathlon (discus, long jump, foot races, wrestling, and javelin) as well as boxing, wrestling as a single event, and equestrian contests. These events were strictly only for the

Greek populace and any other nationality was restricted to participate in the Games.

It is important to remember that although the Olympic games were an athletics competition, it was also a religious festival held in the honor of the god of thunder, Zeus. As such it was a tradition that on the middle day of the Olympic games that 100 oxen would be sacrificed to Zeus. The athletes that participated in the games would pray to the gods for strength, victory, and good fortune. The athletes and spectators would provide offerings and sacrifices to the gods in the form of produce, sacrificial animals, gifts, and cakes, as thanks for their success and gratitude for the right to participate.

The Spring Festivals of Anthesteria and Mounukhion

Anthesteria was the first spring festival of the Ancient Greek world and was one of the first festivals that the Greek populace practiced in honoring the gods. During this festival, the Greeks would wear garlands and would shower themselves with perfume to symbolize the beautiful smells that the spring solstice brings. The Greeks would also participate in contests and would honor and celebrate Dionysus, the god of the grape harvest, winemaking, and wine, by pouring a libation for him of the last of the wine the Greeks had.

The next major festival in Spring for the Ancient Greeks was Mounukhion, which occurred in the middle of spring to honor Artemis, goddess of the hunt and animals. Participants at this festival would offer cakes with torches stuck inside of them to the goddess Artemis.

However, Artemis was not the only deity honored during this festival. It was believed that April was under the protection of Aphrodite and the month of May was under the protection of Apollo. Due to this, there were hymn-singing contests where both the men and the boy's choirs would compete in honor of the two gods of their respective months. The winner of the contests would win a tripod and would then be offered in the name of the gods in respect to them.

There were two different types of offerings that were associated with the Mounukhion festival which seemingly highlights two sides of the Goddess of Hunt's character. The first offering consisted of a goat that was to be dressed as a girl which would be sacrificed in the name of Artemis. This sacrifice was made to represent the event in which the Athenians killed Artemis's she-bear that entered the goddess's shrine. When the Athenians slaughtered Artemis's she-bear she became infuriated with the Athenian's actions and consulted with her Oracles to relay a message stating that an Athenian must sacrifice their daughter as punishment for their barbaric actions. One Athenian bravely accepted Artemis's demands, however, instead of offering his daughter as a sacrifice he performed a switch at the sanctuary and offered a goat dressed as a girl in his daughter's place. Artemis was satisfied and in return for his brave actions, he acquired the priesthood of Artemis for life.

The second offering that occurred during the Mounukhion festival represents Artemis's affiliation with the moon. The Mounukhion festival always took place when a full moon was present. Round cakes were offered to the goddess as a gift to symbolize the moon. These cakes were known as amphiphontes, which translates to "shining all-round," and in the amphiphontes a dadia (a small torch or candle) was stuck in the middle of the cake. The dadia was in reference to the fact that the amphiphontes would only be offered to Artemis when both the sun and the moon were visible at the same time. The amphiphontes would be offered to Artemis with a special prayer. Many Greeks were not particularly skilled in making animal sacrifices, so instead many opted to make offerings of cakes that were shaped as goats or simply offer Artemis amphiphontes to show their admiration for the

Goddess of the Hunt and the Moon.

The Summer Festivals

In Summer, there were many festivals that were hosted by the Greek populace, however, the first festival was known as Plunteria and was hosted around June. This festival revolved around the washing of the illustrious statue of Athena. In Greece, bathing and washing godly statues was a common custom. The women of Greece would be tasked with the duty of cleaning Athena's temple a few days prior to the start of the festival, this act was known as Kallunteria which translates to "to beautify by sweeping." At the same time as the sweeping, the priest would re-light the candles in the temples to symbolize Athena's eternal flame.

June had another festival known as Skiraphoria which occurred during the season in Greece when farmers would cut and pick the grain. The head priestess of Athena, the head priest of Poseidon, and the head priest of Helios would all band together and go to the Skiron, which according to legend is the location where sewing took place for the time. The priests and priestesses of Athena, Poseidon, and Helios would carry a large white canopy over their heads during the procession of the festival, which was mainly celebrated by women. The festival's purpose was to bring fertility to the populace of Greek women.

To honor the gods and receive good fortune and fertility, Greeks would abstain from sexual encounters for the entire day and women would eat cloves of garlic to make themselves undesirable to men. It was also believed that the Greeks would throw offerings in the sacred caves of Demeter.

The next festival that the Ancient Greeks practiced during the season of summer was known as Panathenaia. This festival was considered the celebration of Athena's birthday and was the day the goddess of wisdom, war, and handicraft burst out of Zeus's skull and was given life.

Although the festival was in honor of the goddess Athena's birthday it was also a festival that was in honor of all the Olympian gods as they were all present for Athena's birth. The festival of Panathenaia was a sacred one and was a feast that Greeks believed the  humans and gods celebrated together. The festival would be held every four years, much like the Olympic Games, and every four years a new robe would be woven by the Greeks and offered as a gift to Athena. The robe would always incorporate a middle stripe that displayed the battle between the Titans and the gods which would symbolize the gods' triumph over the savagery brought upon by the tyrant Titans. Greeks from all over Athens would participate in the festivities and would present Athena with many sacrificial animals, gifts, and, and food.

After the festival of Panathenaia, the Greeks would participate in contests of sport and art for the next three to four days. The winners of the athletic contests would be rewarded with a "Panathenaic amphora," a large vase that contained olive oil that was sourced from the goddess Athena's sacred grove. While the winners of all the artistic contests were given a gilded crown of wild olives and were occasionally awarded prize money.

The Autumn Festivals

At the start of autumn there the Greeks participated in a minor thanksgiving festival in honor of Apollo. This festival was known as Boedromia and was participated by the Ancient Greeks to show their thanks to the god Apollo for being a savior in war.

The next festival to follow in autumn was known as Puanepsia, which was a festival that focused on fruit gathering and was practiced seeking divine blessings for the autumn sowing for the Greek populace. The Puanepsia festival was once again in honor of Apollo as he was the god of the son, but the gods Helios (a lesser-known god of the sun) and Horai (god of the seasons) were also worshiped in this ancient festival.

The Winter Festivals

Lastly, there were the Greek festivals of winter, and they were generally more concerned with raising human spirits and reviving the crops than they were about worshipping the gods to return the summer sun. The Greek deities responsible for good harvest, agriculture, and food were generally the gods that were celebrated and honored. In December, minor festivals were held in honor of Poseidon as he was considered the god that provided protection to the humans during that month. The Greeks held a festival known as Posidea to honor the god of the ocean, Poseidon.

CHAPTER 5
THE GREEK PANTHEON OF MT. OLYMPUS

The Olympian gods of Greek mythology were often referred to as the Greek Pantheon. The word pantheon can be understood as a collective group of gods within a particular culture, for example, there would be the Egyptian pantheon of the Norse Pantheon that would consist of those regions' collective gods. The word pantheon comes from the Greek words pan (all) and theoi (gods), thus suggesting all the gods of a particular group or belief system. The ancient Greeks' pantheon consisted of the Olympian gods, along with other major deities as well as various other minor deities and demigods.

The Olympians

The Olympians were the principal deities of Greek mythology and consisted of six gods and six goddesses. These gods and goddesses include

Zeus, Apollo, Ares, Hermes, Poseidon, Hephaestus, Hera, Aphrodite, Athena, Artemis, Demeter, and Hestia.

According to legend, the twelve most celebrated and worshipped gods and goddesses, the Olympians, would spend their days residing on Mount Olympus, the highest peak in all of Greece. Out of the twelve gods and goddesses of Mount Olympus, Zeus was the most important of all, as he was considered to be the king of Olympians and was known to reign supreme over all known beings of the universe, including all of the major and minor deities. Zeus was all-powerful and was responsible for being the protector of justice, kingship, authority, and social order in the universe in its entirety.

The gods, particularly the Olympian gods, played an integral role in the Greek view of the world. The gods were seen as representations of the most significant ideals and features of the human condition and would represent aspects of life such as wisdom, beauty, justice, knowledge, music, and even the changing of seasons. However, due to the long list of the Greek Pantheon, we will highlight the most significant Olympian gods.

Zeus

Zeus was the son of Rhea and Cronus and the

youngest of his six siblings. Zeus had two brothers, Poseidon and Hades, and three sisters, Hestia, Hera, and Demeter. Zeus was the father of all gods and men alike, and the king of the universe. He ruled over Mount Olympus with his golden throne perched on the highest point of the mountain.

Zeus was a sky god, possessed the power to control the weather, and is able to shape the climate and environmental conditions as he pleased. Zeus can also control lightning and bend it to his whim. It was believed that when Earth was blessed with beautiful weather it was because Zeus was in a good mood and was gracefully bestowing mankind with a gift. However, when Zeus was in a bad mood it was believed he would punish mankind with relentless rain, winds, thunder, and lightning bringing disaster upon mortals. Zeus was considered to uphold justice and balance in the universe, and he would punish anybody who lied or broke an oath and reward those who were honest. Zeus was a fair god, and he always tried to maintain balance in the lives of mortals.

Zeus was believed to be a god that loved to laugh out loud and was relatively carefree. Zeus possessed the entirety of the universe's knowledge and was merciful, just, and extremely wise.

However, Zeus was known to be extremely unpredictable and could have an extremely brutal and cruel side to his demeanor. Due to this, no god could accurately read his true intentions or guess the decisions he would make.

Zeus was known to have love affairs with mortals. Many kings claimed to be descendants of Zeus, claiming their bloodline came directly from the gods. However, although Zeus slept with many women, be it a goddess, Titan, or mortal, he ended up marrying his sister, Hera, the goddess of marriage and monogamy. The marriage didn't stop Zeus' affairs, and he continued to have countless encounters with women.

Zeus was known for his amorousness, and in order to achieve this amorous design that he assumed with so many women of various different races, he would frequently assume the forms of animals to arouse and seduce women. Zeus was believed to take the form of a cuckoo when he ravished his wife Hera, he took the appearance of a swan when seducing Leda, and the shape of a bull when he carried off Europa to go make love to her. Due to Zeus's incredibly active sex life, he fathered an enormous number of children. The most notable of Zeus's offspring were the twin's Apollo and Artemis, Helen, Herakles, Athena, Ares, Hebe, Eileithyia, and many more.

In art, Zeus was almost exclusively portrayed as an incredibly handsome humanoid deity with a neatly trimmed beard and shoulder-length black hair. Zeus was incredibly tall and very muscular with an imposing presence about him that demanded respect. Zeus was often associated with an oak tree, and with regard to illustrations, Zeus was always a stately figure in the prime of his life. There are many symbols and trinkets that are largely associated with the Greek god of lightning. Zeus was almost always portrayed as being accompanied by an eagle along with either a scepter or his iconic lightning bolt. Zeus was also often associated with either a ram or a lion and is often clothed with an aegis (a piece of armor with a shield). Zeus was often also carrying a goat's horn, also known as a cornucopia, as this symbolizes his years as an infant when he was brought up and nursed by the nymph Amalthea.

Hera

Born after Hestia and Demeter, Hera was the youngest daughter and third child born to Cronus and Rhea. Some sources cite her as both the oldest and youngest daughter. While she was born

from Rhea last, when the siblings were freed from Cronus' stomach, Cronus emptied his stomach in the opposite order in which he devoured them. Hera, as the last daughter, would have been freed before the others, making her the oldest sister after her rebirth.

Based on numerous different accounts from various worship centers, it is believed that Hera was an incredibly ancient goddess who even predates Zeus. Hera was so ancient that it is believed that nobody knows the queen of Olympus's official name. The name Hera was actually a title placeholder, which when translated means lady or mistress.

Hera would go on to marry Zeus and was regarded as the queen of all the gods of the Greek pantheon. However, even before she married Zeus, it is believed that she ruled over all the heavens and the Earth and was why she is often referred to as the Queen of the Heavens. Hera was the goddess of marriage and birth; thus the goddess was the symbol of family and was often associated with providing welfare for mortal women and children. Hera's Roman name was Juno, and thus the month of June was named in honor of her to this day the month of June is still the most popular time for weddings. Hera and Zeus would have seven children together—Ares,

Eileithyia, Hebe, Hephaestus, Eris, Angelos, and Enyo. However, although they had many children together, their marriage was not a happy one. Hera was known to be incredibly jealous of her husband Zeus' extramarital affairs. She would occasionally punish the women seduced by Zeus out of jealousy.

Zeus was a cruel and brutish husband. When she couldn't bear the mistreatment any longer, Hera plotted a revenge plan with her brother Poseidon and the goddess Athena, possibly even a few other cohorts. Hera drugged her husband, and while all others involved bound Zeus to his bed, stole his thunderbolt. However, Thetis (the goddess of water) managed to summon the hecatonchires Briareus to quickly untie Zeus. Zeus was merciless with his punishment for Hera for her role: he hung Hera from the clouds and attached unimaginably heavy anvils to her feet. Hera, desperate to grant herself release from her excruciating punishment, swore to never challenge or rebel against Zeus again. Instead, Hera would turn her anger and hostility toward Zeus's offspring and lovers.

The most notable of Zeus's offspring who fell victim to Hera's jealousy and wrath was Herakles. The son of Zeus and a mortal woman, and ironically named in Hera's honor, was a target for

Hera on many occasions. Hera sent snakes to kill Herakles as an infant, she raised a treacherous storm to drive Herakles off his course at sea to kill him, and she sent multiple gods with the orders to murder Herakles and those who refused would pay for it severely. Hera was a jealous god who was extremely powerful and vengeful, killing many of Zeus's lovers. Hera was so vengeful that Zeus himself was terrified of her at times.

In art, Hera was generally portrayed as a beautiful, matronly woman. She was often fully clothed with a wreath or a veil and cylindrical crown polo perched on her head. Hera would often be portrayed carrying a scepter that was capped with a pomegranate and a cuckoo. The cuckoo was a symbol of fertility in Greek mythology and is the animal form Zeus took to woo his wife. Hera was also sometimes accompanied in art by a peacock, which was the sacred animal of the goddess of marriage.

Apollo

Apollo was considered one of the most important and complex gods in the Greek pantheon. Apollo was the son of Zeus and the Titan Leto. He was also the twin brother of Artemis, the goddess of hunting. Apollo was associated with many aspects of the human condition, namely truth, prophecy, healing, disease, crops, herds, archery, music, dance, and poetry. Apollo was also considered the most Greek of all the gods. He was known to bring ill health with his arrows, but also could heal epidemics. Apollo has a deep connection to art and was also known to be the muse of many artists and composers. A primary symbol of Apollo is the lyre, a string instrument, as he was said to have created string music. Apollo was also credited, along with his sister, to have invented archery. To add to this impressive resume, Apollo was also associated with the sun and light.

Apollo's nature and temperament are obscure, as, during the time of Homer and onwards, he was considered the god of divine distance. Ultimately, this meant that Apollo would make mortals aware of their own faults and guilt, but would also assist mortals in healing these faults. Apollo would also preside over the religious laws of mortals and oversee the justness of the constitutions of cities. Apollo was known to communicate his knowledge to the mortals of Earth as well as relay the will of Zeus down to Earth. It was said that even the gods were intimidated by Apollo's presence and that only his parents could feel comfortable in his presence.

In art, Apollo was often portrayed as a beardless youthful man, who often appeared naked. In most depictions of Apollo, he would be accompanied by his iconic symbols, a bow, and a lyre. The bow would symbolize distance, terror, and death. On the other hand, the lyre symbolizes Apollo's gentle side and represents the joy of music, poetry, and dance that the gods shared with the mortals.

Artemis

Artemis was the twin sister of the god Apollo and the daughter of Zeus and Leto. Artemis was a widely celebrated goddess and was one of the most important goddesses in Greek mythology. Artemis was primarily known as the goddess of hunting, however, she was also credited as being the goddess of all wild animals, chastity, childbirth, and vegetation.

Artemis was especially popular among the

rural population of Ancient Greece as she brought them good fortune in terms of crops and game to hunt. In the rural population of Greece, it was believed that Artemis was the favorite of all the Greek pantheons. Artemis was believed to be a goddess who loved and adored nature, she was carefree, and she would dance in the company of nymphs in the mountains, forests, and marshes.

Although Artemis was the goddess of hunting, she did not only kill the game, but she would also protect it and nurtured it, punishing anybody who disrespected nature. Artemis was especially protective of the young animals and was given the title by the poet Homer as the mistress of animals.

In art, Artemis was often portrayed as a young woman in her prime around the age of 16-17, she is generally very fit, and a fleet of feet. The goddess is often wearing a knee-length tunic which leaves her legs free to run through the woods without restrictions. Artemis was very athletic and spent most of her time roaming the woods and forests of Earth. She was a very beautiful woman, however, the exact detail of her appearance and the forms she takes on often vary.

Some of the depictions portray Artemis as a woman with multiple breasts so that the goddess of the wilderness could feed a litter as opposed to a single baby or twin offspring. However, it was believed that Artemis remained a virgin and was unable to bear any children of her own. Artemis' divine powers, appearance, and apparel are believed to be a result of six wishes she asked Zeus to bestow upon her when she was just a child. These wishes included ruling the mountains areas of her domain, having more names than her twin brother Apollo, bringing light to the world, inheriting an archery bow and hunting tunic that was crafted by the Cyclopes, inherit sixty nymphs to act as attendants for her hounds and to never marry throughout existence.

Hermes

Hermes was the son of Zeus and Maia, a daughter of the Titan Atlas and nymph Pleione. Often referred to as the "bringer of grace," "the luck-bringing god," or "the slayer of Argus," Hermes was primarily known as the messenger of the gods. He was a psychopomp, a guide for the dead, and as such, transported the souls of the dead and fallen to the king of the Underworld, Hades.

Hermes was more than just a psychopomp and messenger, he was also the patron god of traveling and travelers, the god of fertility, the bringer of sleep, the ruler of dreams, the god of thievery, and a trickster deity. As both the god of sleep and messenger of the gods, people would offer their last libations to Hermes before bed.

Zeus also decided that Hermes would play the role of God of commerce and music. Hermes was credited with the invention of many devices in relation to Greek mythology; it was believed that Hermes was known to invent many musical compositions, including the string instrument kithara, and the fire itself.

Hermes was also known as the god of good fortune and would sometimes provide mortals with gifts. Treasures that were casually found by mortals and any stroke of good luck were considered a gift from Hermes. He was both a helpful god but also associated with trickery and theft. Other gods viewed him as a thief.

In art, Hermes was often portrayed as a young man in his prime who would wear traveling clothes as well as his symbolic winged flat hat known as petasus. He would also wear winged sandals on his feet as well as be depicted with wings on his shoulders. Hermes would generally be shown holding a caduceus, a winged staff with intertwined snakes. This staff would help him gain access to anywhere in the world. He would also often be depicted with an erect or semi-erect penis in sculptures to symbolize his connection of being the god of fertility.

Aphrodite

Aphrodite was the Greek goddess of love, sex, beauty, and fertility. Aphrodite was considered to be the most beautiful of all the gods and the most beautiful specimen in the universe. Aphrodite's name actually originates from the Greek word aphros which translates to "foam." Aphrodite burst  forth from the seafoam caused by Cronus throwing Uranus' genitals into the sea. Due to this, Aphrodite is also considered to be the goddess of the sea and protector of those that travel her waters.

Although Aphrodite represents such a soft, gentle, and beautiful aspect of the human condition, she was also considered to be the goddess of war, especially in the regions of Sparta, Thebes, and Cyprus. However, what Aphrodite was known most for was being the god of love, beauty, and fertility and was believed to occasionally preside over mortal marriages. Aphrodite's circle of worship was generally very formal and was often very strict. What is interesting about the goddess of beauty is that she actually had a large following among the prostitutes of Ancient Greece who considered

Aphrodite to be their patron. This is quite contradictory to the rest of her formal and strict worshipping circles throughout Ancient Greece.

Aphrodite was married to the blacksmith God, Hephaestus, however, this was not a happy marriage and Aphrodite was known to have several other lovers, most notably with the god of war, Ares. Perhaps Aphrodite's promiscuity and her association with sex is the reason she had a large following of Greek prostitutes.

Although Aphrodite was worshiped and honored throughout Ancient Greece, unlike her lover, Ares, there were regions that celebrated the goddess of love and beauty more intensely. The regions where Aphrodite's main center of worship circles was situated are Paphos and Amathus. Amathus is on the small island of Cythera, where it is believed among scholars that the worship of the goddess of beauty originated. Paphos, on the other hand, is situated in what is today known as Cyprus. However, within the main Greek inland, the goddess's chief center of worship was in Corinth.

In ancient Greek art, Aphrodite was often portrayed as a fully clothed woman. It was only in the 5th-century B.C.E. that Aphrodite would gain individualistic features and aesthetic characteristics at the hands of Ancient Greek sculptors. Before the 5th century B.C.E., the artistic portrayals of Aphrodite would lack distinguishing features that would separate the goddess of beauty from the rest of the goddesses of the Greek pantheon. Her most famous sculpture, a full-scale nude sculpture of the beautiful goddess, was carved by Praxiteles. Aphrodite is often described in the literature as having beautiful skin that had absolutely no blemishes or flaws. Aphrodite was also described as having strawberry blonde hair that was so beautiful it was unparalleled to any being in the universe.

The goddess of beauty is often portrayed in art in her early 20s, and was quite tall in stature, possessing a curvy and sexually desirable figure that overwhelmed mortals and gods alike with lust. Aphrodite's neck is often described as being very soft and tender. The goddess of beauty was often known to wear only the finest clothing and don the most lavish of jewelry.

Poseidon

Poseidon was the god of the ocean, storms, horses, and earthquakes. The name Poseidon was derived from the Greek work πόσις (posis) which can be translated to the words "husband or lord" the other part of the god of the oceans' name is derived from the Greek word δã (da) which translates to "Earth." Thus, when Poseidon's name is translated in full it can mean one of two things: "husband of the earth" or "lord of the water."

Poseidon was one of the five siblings of Zeus and was the second-born son of Rhea and Cronus. Poseidon was married to the sea nymph Amphitrite. Poseidon had many offspring with many consorts, his most notable children were Orion, Pegasus, Atlas, and Triton.

Zeus was not the only god of the Greek pantheon to be associated with an iconic weapon. Many of the Greek pantheons had their favored weapons. For Poseidon, he was closely associated with his iconic trident, gifted to him by the Cyclopes to help the Olympian gods defeat the Tyrant rule of the Titans. Just like Zeus's lightning bolt, this Trident was pivotal to the Olympian's victory over the Titans. Poseidon would later go on to use the trident as a tool to rule over the world's oceans. Although Poseidon was the god of the ocean, it was all up to chance that he was given this responsibility. According to legend, once the gods beat the Titans the world was divided into three parts, these being the skies, the oceans, and the Underworld. Zeus and his brothers Poseidon and Hades would go on to draw straws to decide who would rule which part of the newly divided world. Legend says that Zeus drew the straw that represented the skies, Hades drew the straw for the Underworld, and Poseidon drew the straw for the Oceans. From that point on the brothers would rule their allocated part of the new world.

Out of the famed Greek pantheon, Poseidon was one of the most powerful and even the most feared gods of Greek mythology. Many ancient Greeks, particularly sailors, feared Poseidon because he was considered to be the worst-tempered, greediest, and moodiest god of all the Greek pantheon. It was said that Poseidon would often take his fury out on mortals by creating treacherous sailing conditions leading to many Greek sailors' deaths. However, Poseidon was not only feared by mortals, but even Greek deities were fearful of the god of the ocean. It was believed that Poseidon could be incredibly vengeful and hostile towards anybody around him, especially towards mortals, when he was insulted.

However, although Poseidon was known to bestow his wrath on the humans of Earth, he had many heated disputes and run-ins with other gods of the Greek pantheon. As mentioned earlier, Poseidon even went as far as to try and murder his brother Zeus by aiding Hera in her exploits, but that was just one of many occasions he acted hostile and violent towards the gods.

Poseidon was a greedy god and that greed

led him to obsess over the city of Athens, Athena's main city. As a result, Athena and Poseidon clashed. Poseidon claimed that the great city of Athens would benefit more if he became ruler as opposed to Athena. However, it was clear Poseidon had no interest in Athens, he just wanted it for selfish gain. To prove that he would be the greater protector, Poseidon struck a rock with his trident, which produced a beautiful stream of water that encircled the Temple of Erechtheion on the north side of the Acropolis. Poseidon believed that his gift of water would provide the mortals with a source of life in which they could better sustain themselves. However, in reply, Athena planted an olive tree. The gods asked the first king of Athens, Cecrops, to decide who he felt should rule over Athens as their protector. Cecrops decided that Athena's gift of the olive tree would prove more useful as it would provide the citizens of Athens with wood, oils, and fruit, rather than only water. Athena kept Athens, and to this day the olive branch is considered a universal symbol of peace. However, Poseidon never forgave Athena and held an eternal grudge toward the goddesses.

In art, Poseidon was often depicted similarly to Zeus, with a dense beard and long curly hair, and piercing eyes. According to Homer, Poseidon's shriek was as loud as ten thousand men screaming at once. Often Poseidon was portrayed as riding on a four-horse chariot over the waves of the ocean while wielding his iconic trident. Although Poseidon's trident was his most recognizable symbol, it was not exclusive to him as his son, Triton also wielded it.

It was believed that Poseidon used his trident to create the very first horse by striking a rock. The god of the Ocean also used his trident to break off a piece of the Greek mythological island Kos and create the island Nisyros.

Athena

Athena was one of the major goddesses of Greek mythology. She was primarily known as the goddess of wisdom and war but was also associated with agriculture, weaving, spinning, navigation, architecture, and needlework Athena was truly a well-celebrated goddess and was among one of the most respected and admired figures in all of the Greek pantheon.

The birth of Athena is quite remarkable and was an epic tale in itself. Athena was said to have emerged as a fully grown goddess out of the skull of Zeus, however, there is an interesting backstory to this. As we know, Zeus had many lovers and one of his lovers included Metis, an Oceanid nymph. A romantic union commenced between Zeus and Metis, resulting in the Oceanid nymph falling pregnant. Zeus became weary of his unborn child and remembered the danger that he posed to his father, Cronus, as well as, how Cronus posed a threat to his father Uranus. Zeus became troubled and he became increasingly wary that history would repeat himself thus in an effort to ensure that Athena would not overthrow him in the future he swallowed his nymph lover Metis.

However, Metis was still pregnant with Athena and deep within the darkness of Zeus's interior, Metis continued to carry the child. Much time had passed and Zeus was beginning to suffer from terrible headaches. The headaches were becoming unbearable, so Zeus called upon the god of blacksmiths, Hephaestus (some myths say it was Prometheus instead of Hephaestus), to split his head open. Hephaestus agreed and split the King of the Olympians' skull open. Out of Zeus' skull emerged the fully grown Athena in all her glory. Since that day Athena was a proud member of the Olympian gods and goddesses and played an integral role in Mount Olympus.

Although Athena was the goddess of the war, she was very different from her half-brother, Ares. Athena was not associated with the same degree of brutality, violence, or bullying behavior as Ares was, instead Athena was more of a strategist. She was a diplomat who was often summoned by the gods to mediate several disputes and wars amongst the Greek pantheons. Athena was not known to own weapons of her own, but rather known to borrow her weapons from Zeus.

Athena is the patron goddess of the Greeks capital, Athens, and was named in the goddess' honor. In Athens, the goddess' most famous statue stands on the Parthenon. The goddess Athena was responsible for overseeing all of the physical buildings and structures throughout Greece, not only in Athens. She oversaw that these structures would protect the Ancient Greeks from danger and bring prosperity to the lives of the Greek populace. These structures included fortresses, harbors, and even courts of law.

According to legend, the goddess of wisdom and war was believed to play a pivotal role in the Trojan War and opted to side with the Greeks. Athena was also believed to have assisted many demigods and Greek heroes such as Perseus, Jason, Odysseus, and Hercules. In one instance, Athena gave Perseus the gift of a mirror-like shield that would prove pivotal in Perseus's battle against the Gorgon Medusa. Prometheus was also under Athena's tutorage and was taught architecture, astrology, mathematics, medicine, and navigation by the Greek goddess.

In art, Athena was portrayed as a beautiful, tall woman with golden blonde hair. She was

generally portrayed with a physically fit physique and had an athletic build. The goddess of wisdom and war was generally portrayed as clothed in a full set of armor and accompanied by a sword and a shield. Sometimes instead of a shield, she would be wielding a spear. Athena had many symbols that represented her, these included an owl, an olive branch or tree, a clock, a tiger lily, and, occasionally, a lance. In artistic portrayals of Athena, she was generally accompanied by one or a few of these symbols.

CHAPTER 6
THE MANY LARGER THAN LIFE FIGURES OF GREEK MYTHOLOGY

Greek mythology has many other important figures beyond the Olympian gods. There are many other minor gods, demigods, creatures, and other mythical beings that bear great importance in history and culture. Each one has these fascinating creatures and deities have their own myths and lore attached to them. Demigods such as Herakles, Achilles, Theseus, Helen of Troy, and Perseus all make up a significant portion of ancient Greek mythological tales. These demigod's actions are responsible for unfolding major events in Greek mythology and were widely revered and celebrated among the Greek populace. Creatures and minor deities such as nymphs, centaurs, and satyrs are fascinating in their own right and truly give depth to the mythology we all know and love.

Nymphs

Nymphs, also known as nymphai, were any minor goddesses which were associated with nature in one way or another. Nymphs could only be female and were largely considered a class of inferior female divinities. The nymphs populated the earth mainly in the wilderness, wild plains, and forests. Although the nymphs were considered to lie beneath the gods on a hierarchical scale, they were still summoned to grace the presence of the gods and attend all of the assemblies the gods would host on Mount Olympus. The nymphs were responsible for watching over and ruling all sorts of different natural phenomena such as the clouds, the natural springs, the meadows, the beaches, the caves, the trees, and much more. The nymphs were also considered to be the responsible entities for ensuring the well-being and care of all the plants and animals in their domain. Due to this, the nymphs were especially close to the Olympian gods who were associated as being gods of nature such as Hermes, Artemis, and Poseidon.

Nymphs were also associated with fertility, good harvest, and water. Nymphs, unlike other gods and deities, were not immortal. They could die, however, they tended to live exceptionally long lives. Nymphs were distinguished between the spheres of nature in which they represented. There were many different spheres, however, it is important to highlight the major spheres to which the nymphs were connected. The Oceanids were sea nymphs who inhabited only saltwater, while Nereids were nymphs that could inhabit both freshwater and saltwater. Other spheres of nymphs included the Naiads who would watch over and protect the springs, rivers, and lakes. The Oreads were nymphs who presided over the mountains, while the Napaea and Alseids were nymphs who protracted the glens and groves of Earth. Lastly, there were the Dryads, also known as Hamadryads, who would preside over all the forests and trees across the world.

Centaurs

Centaurs, otherwise known as kentauroi, are mythical creatures in Greek mythology who are half-man and half-horse. These unusual creatures were believed to have lived in the mountains and forests of the region known as Thessaly. Ancient Greeks believed centaurs to be primal creatures who would exist in tribes and make their homes in caves. They were also believed to be hunters who would hunt wild animals and arm themselves with spears made of tree branches and sharpened rocks at the tip.

There are many origin myths that surround the legacy of these hybrid creatures, one of these myths says that the mortal King Ixion's son,

Centaurus, fornicated with a cloud nymph by the name of Nephele. It is said that Nephele was created by a jealous Zeus who created the nymph in the image of his wife, Hera. Centaurus impregnated Nephele and as a result, the cloud nymph gave birth to a flock of centaurs. However, this is just one of the many origin stories of the mythical beasts.

Centaurs were believed to have been followers of the god of wine, Dionysus. The Centaurs earned the reputation, just like the god they followed, as being rowdy, boisterous, and savage creatures. According to legend, the centaurs were governed by their animal half as opposed to their human half, and as a result, were bestial in nature. Centaurs were creatures that were believed to be representative of chaos and barbarism. These traits of the mythical creatures were frequently described in Greek sculpture, stories, myths, art, and pottery. However, although these beasts boasted a barbaric and chaotic reputation it was believed that centaurs would only display these treacherous traits when they had consumed alcohol. This could simply have been a metaphor the Greeks would tell to act as a cautionary tale of the barbaric tendencies alcohol can unleash in man if alcohol was used irresponsibly.

According to myth, the centaurs were invited

to attend the wedding of Pirithous, who was the King of Lapith, and who also happened to be the centaur's half-brother. It is said that the centaurs got uncontrollably drunk at the ceremony and tried to carry female guests back home with them. One centaur tried to even carry off the bride. However, the demigod Theseus was also present at the wedding and aided King Pirihous in battle in which most of the centaurs were slain.

The most famous of all the centaurs was known by the name of Chiron. Chiron was considered the most civilized centaur and incredibly wise. His wisdom was so great he tutored and advised many legendary demigods including Achilles, Jason, and HeraklesHerakles. Chiron's family is interesting, to say the least. Chiron was the son of the tyrant Titan, Cronus, and an ocean nymph, Philyra. Thus, he was technically the half-brother of Zeus and many other prolific Olympian gods and goddesses. Chiron married the nymph Chariklo and lived in the deep forest of Mount Pelion.

Although a minor figure in Greek mythology played a big role. Chiron was responsible for the demigod Achilles' education and gifted Achilles with a Pelian ash spear, which Achilles would famously use in the Trojan War. What is more intriguing about Chiron was that he would never drink, thus, according to some legend, would not give in to his bestial nature. Chiron was also not part of the same lineage as the other centaurs and is believed by many to be the very first centaur ever birthed.

Satyrs

Like centaurs, satyrs are also hybrid creatures who are interesting characters in Greek mythology. Satyrs were half-man and half-beast who inhabited the forests and hills of Earth. They are generally depicted as having a human upper body and below their waist, they have the hooved legs of a horse or a goat. They were also believed to have pointed ears and horns protruding from their forehead.

Satyrs were the offspring of mountain nymphs and goats or horses, thus explaining their appearance. However, some legends say that satyrs were the sons of Hekaterides, which were five nymphs who were associated with a popular dance that was practiced in rural areas of ancient Greece.

The ancient Greek poet Hesiod described the

satyrs as brothers of the nymphs. His words held strong credibility with regards to the beliefs of ancient Greek society as his range of influence in Greece was immense. Hesiod would go on to describe the satyrs as "good-for-nothing" and "mischievous" creatures. The satyrs, like the centaurs, were also known to be the followers of the god of wine, Dionysus. Thus, because the satyrs were always in an environment where alcohol was abundant, they had a reputation for brutishness and drunkenness, just like the hybrid centaurs.

Satyrs were not all the same in grand design and as such there were different categories of satyrs. The panes were satyrs that had the legs of goats and were considered to be associated with the god Pan. Although these satyrs differ ever so slightly from other satyrs in appearance, they were sometimes considered in some regions of Greece to be separate from the species of satyrs completely. Another variant of the satyrs included the seilenoi. The seilenoi were older versions of satyrs and would often be depicted as having fat stomachs and long white hair. The seilonoi were often known to be in the company of the god of wine, Dionysus, and were talented in both winemaking and art. The last variation of satyrs included the tityroi. These were the bards of the satyr community and were known to play musical instruments known as a shepherd's pipe. The tityroi were considered to be the local satyrs of the island of Crete.

Demigods

Demigods were the offspring of a mighty deity and a mortal, thus they were half-gods. Demigods were renowned by the Ancient Greeks as entities that were incredibly courageous and strong. Many of the Olympians and other Greek gods, like Zeus, were known to get involved in love affairs with humans and as a result of this union, many demigods were birthed. As demigods were half-man and half-god, it was believed that they possessed great power, strength, and abilities and are often regarded as being as powerful as many of the deities within the Greek pantheon. The demigods were the heroes of the Ancient Greeks and were inherently famous for all that they represented. Demigods such as Herakles, Theseus, Perseus, and Achilles were highly regarded among the Greek populace. Thus, the gods were not the only heroes of Ancient Greece, as the legendary tales about demigod heroes and heroines whose exploits still thrill us to this day. There are many myths and epic tales surrounding the demigods of Ancient Greece. Most of these stories were documented in the famous writings of the Iliad and the Odyssey which were written by the legendary Greek poet Homer. There were many Demigods but the most famous ones included Herakles, Achilles, Theseus, Perseus, and Helen of Troy.

Herakles

Herakles is better known by his Roman name, Hercules, thanks in part to the famous Disney movie of the same name. While that is how we remember him now, we will continue to call him by his Greek name here.

Herakles was a Greek hero in ancient times and quite possibly the most famous demigod in the modern world. Herakles was the Son of Zeus and the mortal Alcmene. He was also the nemesis of Zeus's wife, Hera, and would often be persecuted and attacked by the goddess due to

Hera's jealousy. However, Herakles would always come out on top. Herakles was renowned for always being too powerful for his foes and is known best for his fantastic feats of strength and courage.

One of the more famous tales involving Herakles was the 12 labors. After being driven mad by Hera, Herakles brutally killed his sons and wife. Once Herakles realized the severity of what he had done, he asked Apollo how he could repent. The Oracle of Apollo, Pythia, told Herakles if he really wanted to atone for his sins, he should go and serve his cousin, King Eurystheus, for twelve years. Eurytheus was not a fan of his cousin Herakles and sent the demigod on twelve seemingly impossible labors that no other man would even dare to attempt.

Herakles' 12 labors would be impossible for lesser heroes but for the son of Zeus, nothing could shatter his determination and courage. Herakles' amazing feats of strength and daringness during his 12 labors included slaying the nine-headed sea-serpent, the Hydra, and stealing the girdle from Hippolyta (the queen of the Amazonians), taming Hades' three-headed hellhound Cerbeus, and slaying the Nemean lion.

One of the Parerga (a collection of philosophical reflections) depicts Herakles' battle with a centaur by the name of Nessus. It is thanks to this battle that the Greek hero would meet his demise. The Parerga depicts a scene in which Herakles was traveling with his wife, Deianira. During the couple's travels, Herakles encountered a raging river and a sly, deceitful centaur named Nessus. The centaur offered to help Deianira across the river and Herakles accepted his offer as he saw no harm in his proposal. The centaur helped Deianeria across the river and forced himself on her. Herakles was filled with rage and slew the centaur with an arrow. With the centaur's last breath, he told Deianira that if she smothered Herakles with his blood, Herakles would be forever loyal to her. Deianeira listened to the centaur and saved some of his blood to use on Herakles if she needed it.

Some time passed and Deianeira believed that Herakles was unfaithful to her. Not thinking clearly, she remembered the words of the centaur. Deianeira overwhelmed with jealousy at the thought that Herakles might have another lover other than her, smothered Herakles in his sleep with a tunic smeared in the blood of Nessus. However, the blood did not make Herakles loyal to her. Instead, the centaur's blood poisoned Herakles, forcing the Greek hero to live the rest of his days with the pain of a living fire burning inside of him constantly. Nessus's deceit caused

Deianeira to sentence Herakles to a life of unimaginable agony. Herakles could not bear the pain and pleaded with his father Zeus to take his life. Zeus accepted and killed his son. Upon death, Herakles was brought to Mount Olympus to live the rest of eternity with his father and the other Olympians.

Achilles

Achilles is yet another highly celebrated Greek demigod. Achilles' father was the mortal king Peleus, who ruled over the Myrmidons and the Nereid. His mother was the sea nymph and minor goddess, Thetis. Achilles was considered the most handsome, bravest, and elite warrior of the Agamemnon army who fought in the Trojan War.

Achilles was one of the most famed and respected demigods of the Greek world and it is no surprise that many myths and legends surround the legacy of the Greek hero. Achilles was believed to be almost indestructible. He was the perfect warrior that could not be wounded and was known to have no weaknesses, except for one. Achilles' almost full-proof invulnerability came from a story when Achilles was no more than a baby. It is said that his mother, Thetis, dipped the infant Achilles into a magical river, known as the River Styx. The River Styx would grant the demigod invulnerability to whatever part of the body was submerged underwater. The infant Achillies was fully submerged in the river except for his heels where his mother Thetis held him. Thus, every part of Achilles was invulnerable and could not be wounded except for his heels which would become his only weakness. Achilles' weak heels would become iconic, and to this day the term "Achilles heel" refers to a weakness that a person possesses. This seemingly insignificant weakness would lead to the downfall and death of the famed demigod.

Achilles was a warrior at heart and was one of many great Greek Heroes and demigods that fought in the Trojan War. However, during the iconic Trojan War, Achilles entered into an altercation with Agamemnon, the king of Mycenae. Due to this dispute, the demigod refused to take further part in the Trojan War. Due to this, Achilles decided to give his armor to his cousin Patroclus, who he loved dearly. He felt it would only benefit his cousin in warfare as Patroclus was still fighting against the Trojans. However, fate had been written in blood for Patroclus, and he would die in battle by the hand of a Trojan warrior, Hector. Enraged, Achilles returned to the battlefield and put aside his differences with Agamemnon so that he could avenge his cousin's life. Achilles had his eyes set on revenge and returned to battle the Trojans, where he swiftly killed his cousin's murderer. Achilles made sure to make a statement to the Trojans as he dragged Hector's bloody corpse across the walls of Troy, leaving a bloody trail behind wherever he dragged Hector's body. Achilles did this to show the Trojans his ruthlessness and that he was out for blood. However, in Achilles' rage, he was careless and the Trojans capitalized on the demigods' lack of focus. Achilles was drunk with rage and exposed his only weakness, his heels, and the Trojan warrior Paris saw this as an ample opportunity to kill the almost invincible demigod. Paris shot a perfectly aimed arrow, guided by the god Apollo, striking Achilles' heel. The arrow and shot took the demigod's life.

Theseus

Theseus was the son of the god of the ocean, Poseidon, and the mortal princess, Aethra. Theseus was considered by many Greeks as the greatest Athenian hero Greek had ever known  and he was also known to pull off the impossible by managing to politically unify Attica under the aegis of Athens.

As a child, Theseus was unaware of his divine

origin and was raised by his mother Aethra in the palaces of Troezen. When Theseus reached adulthood, he was told about his origins and how his father was none other than Poseidon. Armed with the knowledge that he was a demigod, he set out to journey forth to Athens. On his journey, Theseus managed to slay and outwit many notorious Greek mythological figures, such as Periphetes (an enormous club bearing Cyclops), the infamous bandit Sinus, Phaea (a giant pig), the outlaw Sciron, Cercyon (the tyrant king of Eleusis), and the bandit Procrustes.

In Athens, Theseus faced much persecution from the goddess Medea, the granddaughter of the god of the sun, Helios. However, Theseus remained untouchable and thwarted all of Madea's attempts to eliminate him. He remained in Athens for several years, during which he would achieve his greatest triumph. Theseus volunteered to be one of fourteen Athenians who would be sent to Crete as a sacrifice to a fierce Minotaur. The minotaur was owned by a king of Crete named Minos and the creature was kept in the confines of a labyrinth. Theseus agreed to be a sacrifice as he knew this would be an ample opportunity to kill the minotaur of Crete within the labyrinth the monster resides in. However, Theseus did not slay the mighty minotaur without assistance. The Cretan princess, Adriane, helped Theseus navigate his way around the labyrinth with a ball of thread. With the help of Adriane's thread, Theseus slew the beast, and set sail back to Athens.

Due to Theseus's triumph in Crete, he was made king of Athens, where he ruled admirably for several years. However, his rule of Athens would be cut short due to an unsuccessful attempt to abduct Persephone from the Underworld. Persephone was the goddess of the Underworld and the daughter of Zeus and Demeter. His voyage to the Underworld resulted in his deposition as King of Athens and the demigod was consequently murdered in torturous fashion by Lycomedes of Scyros.

Perseus

Perseus was an extremely significant figure in Greek mythology. Perseus was yet another son of Zeus and a mortal woman by the name of Danae.

Perseus was sent on an impossible quest by the king of Seriphos. Polydectes sent Perseus to fetch the head of Medusa (a gorgon with wings, a head with snakes in place of hair, and her gaze could turn men to stone). Polydectes sent Persues on this quest thinking it to be impossible to achieve and hoped the demigod would die on his venture. However, the Greek gods intervened and favored Perseus. The Greek pantheon wanted the demigod to succeed on his quest and gifted Persius with magical weapons. The first gift bestowed to Perseus was from Hermes in the form of a curved sword and sandals. Athena provided Perseus with a mirror-like shield. Lastly, to aid Perseus on his epic quest, Hades, the god of the Underworld, gifted Perseus with a helmet that would make the demigod invisible upon wearing it. With these gifts, Perseus was armed and ready to take on any challenge, even a challenge as formidable as the highly dangerous Medusa.

According to legend, the demigod Perseus consulted with a covenant of great witches, known as the Graeae. The Graeae were believed to be three ugly witches who, between the three of them, shared one single eye and one tooth. The Graeae helped Persues to locate the Gorgon Medusa. The Graeae at first were hostile towards Perseus and were hesitant to help Perseus and did not want to tell the demigod the whereabouts of his Gorgon foe. Perseus used his wits and tricked the witches by stealing their one eye and forcing them to tell the demigod where he could find Medusa. The witches knew they had to get their last remaining eye back and were despcrate to have it safely returned to them, so they put aside their hostility and submitted to Perseus's request and told him where he could find Medusa. Once the witches told Perseus where he could find the

Gorgon, he gave the last remaining eye the witches had between them back to the Graeae.

Perseus now knew where to find the Gorgon menace and the demigod ventured forth to slay Medusa in an epic battle. Perseus was able to kill Medusa after a fierce battle but it was largely due to the gifts bestowed to him by the gods. Perseus was victorious. He brought the head of Medusa to Athena, the goddess of war and wisdom, as proof. Perseus later used Medusa's head as a weapon and turned his enemies to stone by forcing them to lock eyes with Medusa's severed head.

Helen of Troy

Helen of Troy is one of the few female demigods in Greek mythology. Helen of Troy's mother was the mortal queen of Sparta, Leda, however, her divine bloodline would come from her father Zeus, who seduced her mother when he took on the form of a swan.

Helen had two siblings, Castor and Pollux. Some myths say Castor and Pollux were also demigods and the sons of Zeus, and according to others, they were simply mortal Spartan warriors. Although what is certain is that Helen of Troy was considered a demigod to the Ancient Greek populace.

Helen of Troy is most famous for the Trojan

War fought in her name and beauty. Helen of Troy was considered so beautiful that some regarded her even more beautiful than the god of beauty herself, Aphrodite. Her overwhelming beauty would lead to her misfortune as she would be abducted by Prince Paris of Troy and forced to become his wife. As a result of Helen of Troy's abduction, war broke loose between the Greeks and the Trojans. It is believed that the gods also were involved in the Trojan War and the Greek pantheon split into factions, some representing the Greeks and some assisting the Trojans.

There were many iconic and significant figures in Greek mythology who took part in the Trojan War such as Ajax, Odysseus, Hector, and Achilles.

The Greek pantheon took a great deal of interest in the Trojan War and found it amusing.

Many gods were believed to have participated in the war and would even choose sides. It was believed that Poseidon, Athena, and Hera backed the Greeks and would assist them where they could. Meanwhile, Ares and Aphrodite assisted the Trojans in their conquest. Many of the Greek pantheons remained impartial to the Trojan War and did not take sides, such as Zeus and Apollo. The participation of the demigods involved in the Trojan War was well documented in the writings of the Odyssey and the Iliad and the legendary war between the Greeks and the Trojans has been etched into history for thousands of years. Finally, after nine years the war came to a halt, and the Greeks came out victorious over their Trojan opposition. Helen of Troy had been rescued and returned to Sparta where she rightfully belonged where she would rule as the queen of Sparta with her husband once more.

CHAPTER 7
GREEK MONSTERS THAT TERRIFIED A NATION AND THREATENED THE GODS

The monsters in Greek mythology were the nemesis of the gods and goddesses and would strike terror in the hearts of the Ancient Greek populace. There are so many monsters within the vast mythology of the Ancient Greeks that it is almost impossible to single out all of them, thus only the most famous and significant monsters will be highlighted and discussed. The monsters made up a significant portion of Greek mythology and were ever-present in the myths and tales of the Ancient Greeks, often appearing in legends regarding epic battles between the Greek pantheon and the ferocious monsters.

Medusa

Medusa was one of three Gorgon sisters. Her sisters were named Stheno and Euryale, however, Medusa was by far the most famous of the sisters.

Interestingly enough, Medusa was the only one of her sisters to not be immortal. It is sometimes said that the goddess Gaea was the mother of the gorgon sisters, however, according to other sources, Medusa's parents were the early sea deities Phorcys and Ceto. However, what mythologists do agree on is that the gorgons were all birthed at sea.

Medusa is generally thought to have been unmarried, however, he was thought to be the lover of Poseidon. Their union resulted in Pegasus and Chrysaor. Pegasus was a winged horse and Chrysaor was the Greek hero who wielded a golden sword.

According to legend, Medusa, at one point in time, was a beautiful woman. She was believed to be a priestess of Athena and made a vow of chastity, however, upon breaking this vow with her lover Poseidon she was cursed. As a result of her affair, Athena punished her by turning the once beautiful priestess into an ugly monster. Athena would turn Medusa's hair into multiple venomous snakes as well as change Medusa's once beautiful skin to a greenish hue. Upon this hideous transformation, it was said that anybody who met eyes with Medusa would turn to stone.

In one of the major myths surrounding the gorgon, the demigod Perseus was sent on a quest to kill Medusa which he was assisted with the aid of gifts by the Greek pantheon. As mentioned in the previous chapter, Perseus was awarded many magical gifts to defeat Medusa one of which was a mirror-like shield, which would prove invaluable in slaying the monster. Perseus managed to fight his foe's reflection thanks to the mirror shield he was given by Athena, and as such defeated the gorgon by decapitating her.

The Hydra

The Hydra was a ferocious monster in Greek mythology and was a formidable foe and posed a deadly threat to the Greek pantheon in many ways. The Hydra was a serpentine beast that donned multiple heads and was one of the guardians of the Underworld. Each one of the Hydra's snake-like teeth contained razor-sharp teeth and he could strike at his foe with all of his heads at once. The Hydra also possessed poisonous breath that would result in immediate death to any human in contact with it. What is worse, though, is that, even if you managed to cut off one of the Hydra's heads, two more would regenerate in its place. He was a truly formidable opponent and so strong that many of the gods were terrified of him. The Hydra did not only have snakeheads but his whole body was snake-like and just like his breath was poisonous it was believed that when he slithered, he would leave a poisonous trail in his wake. The Hydra was large but not as large as one would assume. The Hydra was large compared to other snakes, but he was by no means a giant, in fact, it is said that the beast's body was around the size of an average man, however, with the Hydra's multiple heads he could stand quite tall in stature.

The Hydra was known to reside at the Amymone Spring deep within the Underworld. The Amymone spring was located in a cave and provided the monstrous beast with the protection it needed while it slumbered. The Hydra slept most of its life and would only venture out when it needed to feed. The Hydra was believed to feast on townsfolk and villagers. Due to this, the myth of the Hydra struck fear in rural Greece far and wide.

According to legend, it is believed Hera, Zeus's wife, raised the Hydra with the intention of sending the beast to kill Herakles.

Herakles, as we know, was a demigod who possessed incredible strength and was a formidable foe for any creature. However, Hera was certain that the beast would be enough to end Zeus's son's life. Herakles overheard what Hera was plotting and was also aware of the terror the serpent was issuing upon local villagers and townsfolk. Herakles decided he needed to rid

Greece of the Hydra menace.

Herakles traveled with his nephew Iolaus to kill the serpent once and for all. Herakles drew the Hydra from its slumber by shooting flaming arrows in Amymone Springs's cave. The Hydra, infuriated, launched himself into battle with the Greek demigod. Herakles sliced the many heads of the serpent. Usually, the Hydra's heads would simply grow back, but Herakles' nephew, Iolaus, sealed the Hydra's severed necks shut with a torch preventing them from regenerating. The Hydra, unable to regenerate its heads, only had one head remaining, which Herakles sliced off with one, mighty blow. The Hydra was slain, and Herakles buried the serpent under an enormous rock to ensure the beast would forever be beaten.

Typhon

There were many gods and monsters in Greek mythology, but very rarely was a monster also a god. However, that was exactly the case with Typhon. Typhon was described as the most fearsome and powerful creature in all of Greek mythology and it is no wonder that his very name stirred up so much fear among the Ancient Greek populace.

Typhon was the child of Gaea, the goddess of the Earth, and Tartarus, the murderous bottomless pit of the Earth. According to certain myths, Hera desired to create a god that was even more powerful than Zeus and thus had Gaea and Tartarus mate. It could be argued that Typhon is the product of all the hate that existed in Hera's heart and her jealousy towards Zeus personified.

Typhon was a giant so tall that his head was said to have touched the stars themselves. Typhon possessed a torso of a man, however, his legs were made of vipers which would hiss and attack as the giant slithered. Typhon's head was said to have one hundred snake heads hanging off of it and each one would make the sound of different animals. The monster's eyes were blood red that would glow. Almost anybody who laid eyes on the monster would be stunned in terror. Typhon also possessed a savage jaw, which would breathe fire. The monster's body had over one hundred different types of wings and his hands, like his legs, were made of snakes. Some accounts describe Typhon as a fire-breathing dragon with a hundred heads who would never sleep.

Typhon married Echidna, another half-human and half-snake hybrid. With their union, Typhon was considered the father of all monsters with Echidna as the mother of all monsters. The pair would go on to spawn horrific creatures that would terrorize Greece and bring chaos to the world. Some of their children include Cerberus, the Hydra, the Chimera, the Nemean Lion, Ladon, Caucasian Eagle (the eagle that would eat Prometheus's liver every day for 30 years), and many more.

The greatest myth that surrounds this ferocious monster is undoubtedly his fierce battle with Zeus. Typhon and Zeus had many epic battles. In one of these battles, Typhon destroyed countless cities, threw mountains in his blinding rage, and had his eyes set on demolishing Mount Olympus.  Typhon's brute strength terrified many of the Olympian gods and goddesses. They were so scared of the monster that almost all the gods changed into their animal forms and fled from Mount Olympus. Only Dionysus, Athena, and Zeus stayed in their regular godly forms. Athena, at one point in the battle, called Zeus a coward. This enraged Zeus to an unimaginable level. Zeus attacked Typhon before the monster could destroy Mount Olympus to show Athena that he was not a coward. It is said that Zeus attacked Typhon with one hundred lightning bolts which managed to corner the beast in his tracks. Due to Zeus cornering the beast he managed to overpower

Typhon and cast the monster into the bottomless pit of Tartarus. Once Typhon was in the bottomless pit of Tartarus, Zeus entrapped the monster by covering the pit with Mt. Etna so that the beast would never be able to escape again.

It was believed that all volcanic eruptions were a result of Typhon trying to escape his prison of Tartarus and the lava that erupted was the fire that the monster would breathe. However, it is important to note that this battle was the last of many battles. Typhon and the Greek gods engaged in a ten thousand year war and thus Zeus only managed to end the war thousands of years later by trapping the monster in the same pit that was half responsible for his birth.

Cerberus

Cerberus, also known as the hound of Hades, was a vicious three-headed hound that guarded the gates of the Underworld. He made sure that the spirits of the dead were allowed to enter the Underworld but were never allowed to leave. Cerberus was a child of Typhon and Echidna (half-woman and half-snake) and was part of a ferocious family of monsters which included the Hydra, the Chimera, and Orthus. Upon guarding the gates of the Underworld, the monstrous hound would only be tricked three times. Once by the strength of Herakles, once by the music of

Orpheus, and once by the Sybil of Cumae who tricked the beast with a cake.

To understand Cerbesus one should understand how dogs were perceived in the ancient world. In Ancient Greece, dogs were seen as wild animals who defied domestication. Although many dogs were companions to many Greeks and were often used as guard dogs, there were still many negative connotations attached to their canine companions. Dogs would often roam the streets of Greece in packs and scavenge throughout the town and cause havoc. Thus, Cerbeus was the embodiment of these negative traits that dogs were perceived to possess. However, the monster Cerbeus did not only possess the traits of the fearful qualities of ancient canines but also possessed a mixture of traits from many other feared animals. Thus, Cerberus was an amalgamation of ancient Greek nightmares.

Although Cerberus is often only described as a three-headed dog there was more to it that surrounded this legend. Cerberus was a monstrous dog that had three heads, a serpent's tail, a mane made out of snakes, and the claws of a lion. According to some legends Cerberus's heads were meant to represent the past, the future, and the present. However, other legends suggest the hound's heads represented birth, youth, and old age.

The most famous myth surrounding Cerberus involves the demigod Herakles. Cerberus was the last of Herakles' 12 labors. According to legend, King Eurytheus sent Herakles on a quest to capture Cerberus alive. Eurystheus was certain that this quest would be too much, even for Herakles, and expected the hound of the Underworld to kill Herakles. However, Herakles was convinced he would be successful on his quest. Herakles traveled to the Underworld and proposed a proposition to the god of the Underworld, Hades. Herakles asked Hades if he could take Cerberus out of the gates of the Underworld without the use of weapons and if he would be allowed to freely leave with the canine. Hades, who would generally never allow anybody to leave the Underworld once they have entered, was amused by Herakles' request and granted the demigod permission to leave upon successfully subduing Cerberus.

Herakles found Cerberus on the shores of Acheron and challenged the beast to a wrestling match using only his bare hands. Cerberus agreed to Herakles' challenge and the two began an epic showdown. Herakles had to use every ounce of his strength to subdue the monstrous hound but ultimately prevailed. Even though Herakles was the strongest man in the universe, he still struggled immensely. After a long battle, Cerberus grew weary and ran out of breath due to a devastating chokehold from the demigod. Finally, Herakles loosened his grip knowing that if he continued Cerberus would surely die. Herakles was successful with his quest and brought back the three-headed hound to King Eurytheus as requested. However, later Cerberus was returned to Hades to watch over the gates of the Underworld once more. Cerberus was one of the very few monsters who fought Herakles and survived.

CHAPTER 8
MYTHS THAT WITHSTOOD THE TEST OF TIME AND DEFINED A MYTHOLOGY

The myths of Greek mythology are truly fascinating, however, due to the immense amount of Greek myths out there, it is often overwhelming to know where to begin. Up until this point, many of the Greek myths in the previous five chapters have already been discussed. However, even so, there are so many fascinating Greek takes to be told that there is an arsenal of myths still waiting to be highlighted. Each myth is as fascinating, if not more so than the last. Greek mythology never seems to fail to capture our imagination and provides us with timeless tales that leave us captivated after every read. There are so many Greek myths to uncover, and it is impressive how many of these myths have withstood the test of time.

Pandora's Jar

Pandora's box is a common idiom, taken from Greek mythology. While the idiom refers to a box, in the original myth, it was often portrayed as a jar. This myth takes place after Prometheus gave the gift of fire to the mortals of Earth. As mentioned earlier, Zeus did not take kindly to Prometheus stealing the gift of fire from the gods. Zeus also took vengeance on the mortals; he saw the mortals just as guilty for accepting the gift of fire. Zeus ordered Hephaestus, the god of blacksmiths, to create the first mortal woman out of soil and water as the punishment for the mortals as he knew one day, she would be responsible for unleashing unspeakable evil on mankind. The name of the woman was Pandora. Each god and goddess were instructed by Zeus to give Pandora a gift. Athena gave Pandora the gift of wisdom, Aphrodite gave beauty, Hermes provided Pandora with cunning, and so on until all the gods had given some gift, no matter how large or small, to Pandora. The name Pandora can be translated from Greek to English as "all gifts."

Zeus told Pandora she was to visit Epimetheus, the brother of the punished Prometheus. Prometheus was fearful of Zeus at this point and believed Zeus was trying to harm his brother as a result of Prometheus's forbidden gift of fire. Thus, Prometheus urged his Epimetheus not to accept any gifts from Zeus or be seduced by Pandora, no matter how sincere she may seem. However, Prometheus's brother, Empetheus, accepted Pandora as a gift from Zeus. Empetheus fell in love with Pandora and the pair married. All the gods and goddesses attended the wedding, and on Pandora's wedding night Zeus gave her a gift, just like all the other gods and goddesses before him. Zeus gave Pandora a jar. Zeus had warned the mortal women not to open the jar under any circumstance. However, Pandora was forever drawn to the contents of the jar and could not stay away from it any longer.

Epimetheus kept the key to Pandora's jar safe on his person at all times to ensure nobody would open the jar. However, one night when Epimetheus was sleeping, Pandora stole the key from her husband and opened the jar. Upon opening the jar, all evil was immediately released into the world. When Pandora opened the jar, hatred, war, death, hunger, sickness, and all disaster engulfed the world. Once the jar was opened, the contents could not be returned to it, forever dooming mortals to suffer.

The Myth of Icarus

The tale of Icarus and his father Daedalus is one of the most famous Greek myths. Daedalus was a famous engineer and inventor, said to be taught by Athena herself. A king, King Mino, learned of Daedalus' talent and commissioned him and his son, Icarus, to build a great labyrinth to imprison a deadly minotaur. This is the same minotaur and labyrinth that Perseus would later slay.

Upon Daedalus and Icarus finishing their work on the labyrinth, King Minos imprisoned them inside of it to prevent them from spreading knowledge of the labyrinth or minotaur's existence to the public. Night after night, Daedalus and Icarus tried to come up with ways to escape. One night, Daedalus had an idea. Icarus and his father gathered many feathers from birds and glued them together with wax. With the feathers and wax, Daedalus made four large wings for them to escape the labyrinth.

Daedalus warned his son that the wings were fragile, as they were only held together by wax, and he pleaded with his son to never fly too close to the sun as the wings would melt and he would fall to his death. Icarus told his father not to worry, assuring him that he understood. However, as the two of them were passing the island of Delos, to his delight, Icarus forgot his father's warning and flew too high. The heat of the sun melted the wax, as Daedalus said it would, and Icarus fell into the ocean and drowned. Daedalus was absolutely distraught with the death of his son and named the area "Icaria" in honor of his son.

The Abduction of Persephone by Hades

This myth tells the tale of the abduction of Zeus and Demeter's daughter Persephone and can also be seen as an ancient explanation of how the Greeks understood why certain seasons would blossom and others would not.

The daughter of Demeter (goddess of the harvest and agriculture) and Zeus, Persephone, grew to become an incredibly beautiful goddess and was admired by many. This beauty would ultimately lead to much misery for the goddess as Hades, the god of the Underworld,  saw what a beautiful woman Persephone had grown into and immediately fell in love with her. Hades had become overcome with lust for Zeus's daughter and decided to abduct her and take her back to the Underworld with him. According to Homer, the story begins on a sunny day when the beautiful Persephone was picking flowers in a field with a few of her closest ocean nymph friends. While searching for the most beautiful flower on earth, Persephone moved away from her companions. Persephone found what she was looking for, and as she bent down to pick the extravagant flower, the Earth opened, and out came Hades on his golden chariot. The god of the Underworld snatched Persephone without a second thought and carried Zeus's daughter back to the Underworld while the goddess was in tears.

Demeter was truly distraught about Persephone's abduction and searched across all the known world, day in and day out. Her search was in vain, and Persephone was nowhere to be found. With Perrsephones' absence, the crops and the land of the Earth began to wither away, as the pain of Demeter grew more severe with each passing day her daughter was missing. However, there was a glimmer of hope as there was a witness to Persephone's abduction. The sun had seen what truly happened to Demeter's daughter and felt sorry for the goddess after watching Demeter's painful search. The sun told Demeter the details of Persephone's abduction. Demeter armed with this new information was absolutely infuriated and could not believe what the sun had just told her. In a fit of rage, Demeter marched to her lover and Persephone's father, Zeus, and demanded that their daughter be returned to them at once. As Demeter was the goddess of the harvest and agriculture, she threatened to never let the world blossom again unless Persephone would be returned to her safely.

Zeus listened to his lover's threats and knew that the world could not survive without arable land and thus would demand that Persephone be returned to Demeter at once. Zeus sent Hermes, the messenger god, to demand that Hades release Persephone immediately and if Hades refused, there would be dire consequences. Hades knew that if he were to fight Zeus, he would be no match for his brother and agreed to release Persphone. However, Hades was clever and cunning and had a trick up his sleeve. Hades would force Persephone to eat six six pomegranate seeds from the Underworld before handing over Demeter and Zeus' daughter to Hermes. Hades knew that if Persphone ate food from the Underworld, she could never truly escape. This was because whether a god, mortal, or any being eats from the Underworld they may never leave.

Although Persephone ate the six pomegranate seeds from the Underworld, she was returned to Hermes and was reunited with her parents once more. Hermes told Demeter that Hades forced Persephone to eat the fruit from the Underworld. Not surprisingly, Demeter was absolutely furious and distraught. Demeter knew that anybody who ate food from the Underworld could never leave for a sustained period of time without being severely harmed and thus feared for her daughter's safety. However, Zeus was diplomatic and proposed a compromise. Zeus proposed that for every pomegranate seed Persphone ate, she would spend a month in the Underworld. In other words, for six months of the year, Persephone would live on Mount Olympus and for the other six months, she would live with Hades in the Underworld. Demeter knew she had no other choice and was forced to accept Zeus's proposal. Thus, every six months Persephone would travel to Hades in the Underworld, and during those months Demeter would mourn for her daughter, and the crops and the land would begin to wither. Demeter would ensure the Earth would blossom once again for six months when Persephone would return home to Mount Olympus and live with her mother Demeter and the other Greek pantheons.

The Love Story of Eros and Psyche

This is a myth of love and how love isn't always how we expect it to be. This myth is about the mortal woman Psyche and Aphrodite's son Eros, who is the Greek version of the Roman Cupid. The story begins with Psyche, whose name can be translated to mean "soul" in English. Psyche was a mortal, but she was no ordinary mortal; she

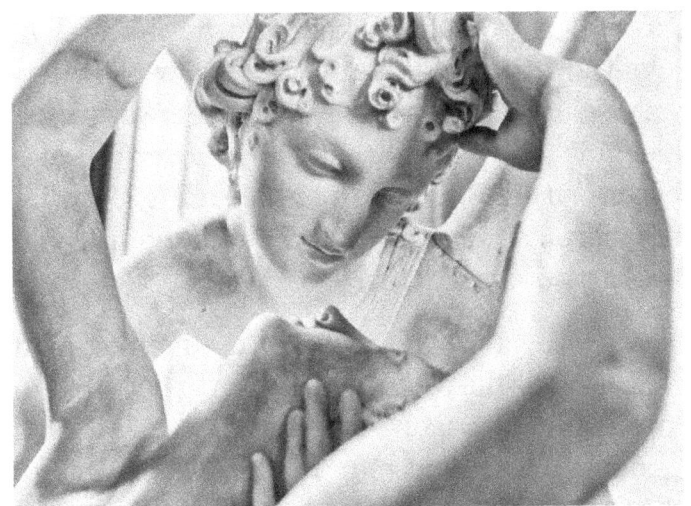

possessed beauty that even the gods and goddesses could not parallel. Many mortal men regarded Psyche to be even more beautiful than the goddess of beauty Aphrodite herself.

Greeks from across the land would travel from far and wide to visit Psyche so they could admire and bask in her beauty. Some men stopped worshipping Aphrodite, as they were too awestruck by Psyche's beauty. Aphrodite was not pleased with this situation and the goddess of beauty became overwhelmed with jealousy and fury directed toward Psyche. The goddess of beauty knew she had to put an end to this and decided to punish Psyche. Aphrodite sent her son, Eros, to ensure that Psyche would fall in love with the vilest and most despicable creature in all the known Greek world. Eros, like the Roman Cupid, possessed arrows that could make anybody fall in love with the first thing that they saw once they were struck with the "love arrows." However, just like how the mortals would swoon over Psyche's beauty, so did Eros and Aphrodite fell in love with the mortal as soon as he saw her and thus could not carry out his mother's task.

Instead, Eros decided to do nothing and refused to be the reason Psyche would be forced to love a hideous creature for the rest of her life. Eros remained silent and returned to the company of the Greek pantheon. Years had passed since Eros last saw Psyche, however, with each passing year Eros's love for the mortal woman grew stronger and stronger. What was truly strange was that Psyche remained unmarried even after all these years had passed, even with her unparalleled beauty and lack of intervention from the gods. It was believed that the Greeks would still admire Psyche's beauty, but none would ask for her hand in marriage, perhaps they were intimidated by such divine beauty. However, men would go on to marry other women, and Psyche with all her beauty would remain unwed. This worried Psyche's parents, and they grew concerned about their daughter's lack of suitors. They were afraid that their daughter would remain unwed for the rest of her life despite her overwhelming beauty.

Due to their concern, Psyche's parents decided to seek the guidance of Apollo to help advise them as to what they needed to do. The oracle who watched over Apollo's temple and spoke on Apollo's behalf told Psyche's parents that there was only one way that Psyche will ever be married. Psyche's parent's ears perked up and they were willing to do whatever it took. The oracle said that Psyche would have to wear a black dress and climb the peak of a high mountain all by herself and wait there. According to the oracle, while Psyche waits on the mountain peak, she will be met by a winged serpent who will take Psyche as his wife. Psyche's parents were horrified about what they were just told, but they were desperate to find a husband for their daughter and believed they had no other choice than to listen to the oracle of Apollo.

The next day, Psyche made her way up the mountain as the oracle told her and waited at the highest peak. While Psyche was waiting at the top of the mountain, she was shaking and crying in fear until, suddenly, the fresh wind of Zephyrus lifted her up and guided her to a magnificent castle floating in the sky. Psyche was confused and frightened, as she had no idea what was happening. At the castle, Psyche was greeted by a soft sweet voice that put her nerves at ease and made her feel welcome and at home.

The voice that she heard was none other than Eros, the son of Aphrodite, who has been in love with Psyche for years ever since he laid eyes on her, but Eros would not expose himself to Psyche, and he was nothing but a voice to the perspective of the mortal woman. However, every night in the castle Eros would lie next to Psyche in the dark, but Psyche would never actually see Eros and thus she did not know who was sleeping beside her every night. Although Psyche never actually saw Eros laying beside her night after night, she could feel that it was not a vile monster laying beside her but rather a caring, loving husband that she and her parents had always wished for.

Days turned into weeks and Psyche was joyous and content with her new life. However, as she was living in the castle in the sky, she was far away from her family and began to miss them. Psyche felt sorry for them as she had left them all alone. She decided to ask her new husband if her family could come to visit her in the castle in the sky where she now resided.

Eros was skeptical at first but finally submitted to his wife's request and accepted her terms. Eros pleaded with Psyche to not be influenced by her family, otherwise, the relationship she has formed with her new, mysterious husband would be destroyed and they both would suffer. The next day arrived and Psyche's two sisters came to visit her in the castle in the sky. Psyche's sisters were carried like she was, by the wind of Zephyrus, to Psyche's new home. Psyche's sisters were incredibly jealous of her, as they believed that Psyche was living a life of royalty and divinity. The two sisters began to laugh at Psyche as Psyche told them that she has never actually seen her husband before. The sister out of jealousy and envy told Psyche that the reason she has never seen her husband was that was in fact the hideously vile monster the oracle of Apollo had prophesied. What Psyche's sisters said to her really hit a nerve and truly overwhelmed the mortal woman. Psyche's sisters left to go back home but their words did not and they lingered in Psyche's mind like a stain that cannot be cleaned. Psyche began to feel truly conflicted and confused as to why after all this time her husband still has not shown his face. Psyche was desperate to find out the identity of her new husband and came up with a plan.

Psyche's plan was that one night, when her mysterious husband was asleep next to her in the dark, she would light a candle to expose the true identity of her husband. She had decided that if the person sleeping next to her every night was exposed to be a monster, then she would kill with a blade. However, if the candle exposed a man she would roll over and happily go back to sleep. Psyche went along with her plan that night. She lifted the candle and revealed it was not a vile serpent or monster, but Eros! Unfortunately, as she lifted the candle over her sleeping husband, a drop of hot oil from the candlestick fell on his cheek of Eros and woke him up. Betrayed, Eros said, "love cannot live without trust." Psyche immediately regretted what she had done and felt horrible for her intrusive actions. Eros ran out of sight and could not be found anywhere. Psyche was desperate to find her husband, and despite the fact that Psyche had only seen his face for the briefest of seconds, she immediately fell deeply in love with him. Psyche was at her wit's end and decided to approach Eros' mother. Although Aphrodite detested the mortal for her beauty, the goddess said she would help Psyche to reunite with Eros if she could complete four seemingly impossible tasks. Miraculously, Psyche was able to  complete these tasks with the help of nature and even the assistance of the gods.

The first task that Aphrodite demanded Psyche to complete was to sort out an enormous stack of wheat, barley, millet, poppy seeds, peas, lentils, and beans that had been mixed together in a heap by Aphrodite. To make this task even harder Psyche only had one day to complete this task. Psyche was overwhelmed and did not have a clue where to even begin, however, fortunately for her a herd of nearby ants felt sorry for the beautiful mortal. These ants managed to secure the help of all the ants across Greece to help Psyche finish Aphrodite's task in time. Psyche completed what had been asked of her, but she still had three more tasks she had to complete.

For Psyche's next task Aphrodite demanded that her son's wife gather a clump of golden wool that could only be acquired from a flock of murderous sheep with dangerously sharp horns. Once again, Psyche was overwhelmed and did not know how she would successfully complete Aphrodite's task. However, nature once again helped Psyche and this time a divinely inspired green reed would advise her. The green reed told Psyche that she must wait till the heat of the afternoon before she attempts to steal the golden wool as this is the time that the sheep would be asleep. Psyche was grateful and listened to the advice of the green reed and returned to Aphrodite with a lapful of golden wool. Aphrodite was still not impressed and demanded that Psyche complete another task.

Aphrodite gave Psyche her third task and this time it was even more complicated. Aphrodite demanded that Psyche was to fill a jar with the fresh waters from the deadly river Styx, which could only be recovered from the water that flowed on the top of a distant mountain. The journey alone was incredibly dangerous, and Psyche went to great lengths to simply reach the river Styx. However, Psyche pushed through and managed to reach the river, although Aphrodite did not tell her what would be waiting at the river Styx. Psyche arrived at the river only to find an enormous dragon who guards the water of the river Styx against intruders. Psyche froze at the sight of the dragon out of fear. Fortunately, Zeus noticed the fear struck Psyche before it was too late and remembered that he owed Eros a favor. In order to pay off his debt to Eros, Zeus sent down an eagle from Mount Olympus to snatch the empty jar from Psyche's hands and fill it with the water of the river Styx before handing the filled jar back to Psyche. Psyche was saved and was successful with her task.

Aphrodite, furious with Psyche's success, demanded that she complete one final task. Psyche was tasked to go to the Underworld and retrieve a day's worth of Persephone's beauty cream and bring it back. However, the only way to enter the Underworld would mean that Psyche would have to die. Psyche was ready to do whatever it took to see her husband again and thus went up one of the highest towers she could find with the intention of jumping off of it so that she could enter the Underworld. However, at the last moment, the tower she had planned to jump off of was inspired by Psyche's motivation and pure intentions that it told her a better way to enter the Underworld. She followed the advice of everything the tower had told her.

She first went to a hill called Taenarus in the Peloponnese, where she would be able to find a hole that would lead her to Hades. However, she would not go empty-handed as she went on her journey with two coins and two pieces of bread soaked in honey and barley. Psyche used the first of her two coins to pay Charon (the ferryman of

Hades) who took her across the river Styx to the Underworld. After Psyche's ride on the ferry, she met Persephone and would refuse any of her meals that she offered her just as the tower had advised her to do. Instead of accepting the food from Persphone, the tower advised Psyche to request a crust of brown bread and a favor. Psyche did just that and asked Persephone for a jar of her beauty cream. Persephone accepted and brought the cream to Psyche as she had asked for. Psyche had got what she came for and returned to Aphrodite by bribing Cerberus to let her out of the Underworld with her honey-soaked bread and paid Charon to take her to the other side of the river Styx with her last coin.

Psyche returned to Aphrodite with all the tasks completed, however, despite Psyche's success, Aphrodite was enraged and yelled at the mortal woman that she would never let her go. The gods of Olympus witnessed this act of injustice and sent Hermes to let Eros know of everything that has happened. Eros loved Psyche and was touched by her love and thus returned to her. From that day on Eros and Psyche had an official wedding and were happily married. All the gods and goddesses attended their wedding and Zeus allowed Psyche to taste the drink of the gods as a wedding gift, granting Psyche immortality. Even Aphrodite was now pleased, as now that Psyche was immortal

mortal men would forget about Psyche and once again praise Aphrodite, the true goddess of beauty.

CHAPTER 9
BATTLES AND CONQUESTS: THE TROJAN WAR AND ALEXANDER THE GREAT

One cannot talk about Greek mythology and Ancient Greece without mentioning the legendary Trojan War and the immense significance Alexander the Great played in the Ancient Greek world. These events are critical standpoints not only in Greek history but in world history. The Trojan war, quite possibly the most famous ancient mythological war throughout history, is an epic tale about how mortals and gods fought together to bring down the city of Troy. While the great conquests of Alexander the Great were not clouded in mythological beliefs, such as the Trojan War, they were the stories of legends themselves. Alexander the Great was an incredibly influential, if not the most influential, figure in all of ancient civilization, and the influences his conquests and united empire bestowed upon the known civilized world were revolutionary, to say the least.

The Trojan War

The Trojan War is a legendary battle and is arguably the most iconic battle in all of Greek history. However, the myth that surrounds this battle and what caused the tension between the Greeks and the Trojans is quite astounding. According to myth, the origin of the Trojan war started with a golden apple and a few envious goddesses. The myth begins with the wedding of Thetis and Peleus, the goddess of discord. According to legend, Thetis and Peleus invited various gods and goddesses of the Greek pantheon but did not invite the goddess Eris, the goddess of strife and chaos. Eris was greatly offended by the disrespect shown by the soon-to-be-married couple and decided to gatecrash the wedding. Eris made a dramatic entrance to Thetis and Peleus' wedding and tossed a golden apple in the middle of the table on which the gods and goddesses were feasting during the ceremony. Eris announced to all the guests of the wedding that the golden apple was meant to be a gift to the fairest of all the goddesses, as she knew this would create conflict and tension among the Greek pantheons. Eris's golden apple was claimed by not one but three goddesses—Athena, Hera, and Aphrodite. However, as the apple was a gift to the fairest of them all, only one goddess could physically eat the apple. This led to a fueled dispute among Hera, Aphrodite, and Athena. The three goddesses argued for hours but they could not decide who the most beautiful goddess was, so they asked Zeus who Eris's golden apple rightfully belongs, However, Zeus decided to take on a diplomatic approach to the situation and decided that he would not choose who the golden apple rightfully belongs to. Although he would instead bestow this honor to Paris, a human male and the rightful Prince of Troy should decide in his place.

Paris was no more than a humble shepherd living on Mount Ida and was oblivious of his royal lineage. Paris had an interesting past, and as a child, he was abandoned by his parents when he was just a baby. This was because an oracle had prophesied that Paris would be responsible for the destruction of Troy, the very city that he is the rightful prince of.

However, it was now up to Paris to decide who out of Hera, Aphrodite, and Athena was the fairest of them all. The three beautiful goddesses appeared before Paris and demanded that he choose who he felt was the most beautiful. Paris was now faced with a daunting task and was overwhelmed with the decision he was expected to make. At first, the rightful Prince of Troy was hesitant and the goddesses noticed Paris's indecisiveness. Each of the three goddesses offered him a gift to entice him to choose them.

First up was Hera, who offered Paris kingly power. The next goddess to offer a gift to the rightful Prince of Troy was Athena, who offered him wisdom and glory among all mortals. And finally, the goddess of beauty, Aphrodite, offered Paris the love of the most beautiful woman on Earth. Based on what the three goddesses had offered Paris, he made his decision with no hesitation. Paris gave Eris's golden apple to Aphrodite and from that day, Aphrodite continuously offered counsel to Paris and led the shepherd to Troy, informing him about his royal lineage and what was rightfully his.

Thus, it can be said that the events of Eris's golden apple were the catalyst to the epic Trojan War because as promised, Aphrodite would secure the "love" of the most beautiful woman on Earth—Helen of Sparta. At the time, Helen of Sparta was considered the most beautiful woman in the known world. She was married to the King of Sparta Menelaus, and it was declared by Aphrodite that Helen of Sparta was to be given to Paris and she was his for the taking. Paris listened to Aphrodite and abducted Helen and would forcefully make her his wife. Paris refused to return Helen under any circumstances to the king of Sparta, Menelaus.

Due to Paris's treacherous acts, the Trojan War was born. The Spartan king, Menelaus, and his brother Agamemnon waged war against the Trojans and gathered an enormous army of Greeks soldiers to sail to Troy. The formidable Greek army that was assembled by Menelaus and Agamemnon would gather at Aulis, a port town in Ancient Greece. According to legend, many of the greatest Greek heroes participated in the Greek army against the Trojans and included demigods and formidable warriors such as Achilles, Patroclus, Ajax, Odysseus, Nestor, and many others. As mentioned earlier in Chapter Four, the Greeks were also aided by many gods, however, other gods were also assisting the Trojans.

The Greek army's ships were not sailing as they should and were standing idle due to the fact that Artemis had refused to provide the wind needed for the fleet to sail. This was because Agamemnon killed Artemis's sacred deer. The Goddess demanded that he pay a price and atone for his sins and if he refused the Greek fleet would not be able to sail. Artemis proposed a compromise and said she would only provide the wind the Greeks needed if Agamemnon sacrificed his daughter, Iphigenia. Artemis demanded an eye for an eye, Agamemnon's daughter's life for her sacred deer's life. Agamemnon agreed, and once the sacrifice was made, granted the wind needed for the ships to set sail.

The majority of the Trojan War was fought as a protracted siege by the Greek army on the city of Troy. According to experts, the war was said to have lasted for over nine years and of those nine years, the Trojans managed to resist the Greek army's invasion of the city of Troy, except for one fatal siege which will shortly be discussed. The reason the Trojans were able to withstand the onslaught of the Greek army was that, according to legend, the walls that surrounded Troy were built by the gods Poseidon and Apollo. This was Apollo and Poseidon's punishment by Zeus many years before the Trojan War due to an act of impiety from the two gods in question. Apollo and Poseidon were ordered by the King of the Olympians Zeus to the Trojan King, Laomedon, for an entire year, during which they built the impressive fortifications of Troy.

Throughout the nine-year battle of the Trojan War, there were many battles between the Greeks and the Trojans, however, they were almost exclusively fought outside of the impenetrable wall of Troy. Most times, the battles were fought by soldiers engaging in battle on foot with swords and shields, although on occasion, battles would be fought with chariots. The Trojan War seemed like there would be no end as for nine years the war waged back and forth across the plains of Troy, and it seemed to be a stalemate Greek Heroes and demigods such as Achilles and company fought valiantly and managed to strike fear in the Trojan's hearts. However, the wall was the Trojans' protection and not even the might of demigods could break down Troy's fortification. The Trojans knew as long as the wall stood, they would be safe regardless of how fierce the heroes of Greece fought. Although the war waged on for nine years, it was the final year of the war that featured the greatest battles and highlights. The ninth year of the Trojan War was the year of the Trojan horse.

As the war waged on, the Greek hero Odysseus had a genius idea that would put an end to the Trojan War and see the Greeks victorious. Odysseus proposed that the Greeks built an enormous, hollow wooden horse and a  small group of warriors would hide within to strike the Trojans when their guard was down. The Greeks loved this idea and were immediately on board with Odysseus's genius strategy. Thus, the Greeks implemented their new flawless plan the next morning. As the Trojans noticed that an enormous wooden horse was standing outside of the gates of Troy, they were confused as they had no idea where this wooden horse had come from. Out of curiosity, the Trojans took the horse within the walls of Troy, despite the warnings of many residents of Troy.

However, the Trojans did not listen to the pleading warnings of their citizens and took the giant wooden horse inside the walls of Troy. The Trojans began to celebrate with music and wine as many thought it to be a gift from the Greeks as a sign of a truce. Little did the Trojans know they were about to be bombarded by an enormous Greek army flooding inside the walls of Troy. When the Trojans went to sleep, the soldiers inside the hollowed-out wooden horse crept out and opened the gates of Troy. With the gates of Troy open, the Greek army could now finally enter the interior of the indestructible wall of Troy. Thus, the Greek army entered Troy without any resistance. The Greeks slaughtered the Trojans with a surprise attack and Troy fell. The battle was not without Greek casualties. The hero Achilles was shot in the heel by Paris, killing him in the battle. Nevertheless, the Greeks won the war, and Helen of Troy was retrieved and returned back to Sparta, where she would rule as a queen with her husband Menelaus.

Alexander the Great of Macedonia

Alexander the Great is one of the greatest figures in world history and it is no surprise that he left an enormous mark on Greek society during his reign. Alexander the Great was born in the year 356 B.C.E. on the 20th of July to King Phillip II of Macedonia in the city of Pella. When Alexander the Great was a young teenager, his father hired the great philosopher, Aristotle, to tutor his son. Through Aristotle's tutelage, Alexander developed a love for science, particularly medicine and botany. However, Alexander the Great was best known for his highly successful reign as a conqueror. Alexander the Great would conquer most of the known civilized world at the time.

Alexander the Great was a man of unparalleled ambitions that were so frightening they even overwhelmed him. He even thought of himself as a god, not a man, due to his accomplishments and ambitions. There were even those that thought he was the son of Zeus, and it's possible that Alexander the Great made this claim himself. He is one of the earliest to have the word "Great" attached to his name. Others would go on to use this title, such as Constantine the Great and Charles the Great, however, no other conqueror managed to personify greatness like Alexander.

Alexander the Great is arguably the most successful and skilled general and conqueror in all of known history. The ruthless general managed to gain control and conquer the Persian army in its entirety. The Persian Empire was an enormous amount of land and the very thought of bringing down the Persian Empire seemed to be an impossible feat, yet this did not stop Alexander the Great from bringing the Persian Empire to its knees. The Persian Empire included a large portion of Asia, Syria, Egypt, Babylon, and of course Persia itself. Along with being history's greatest generals, he was also one of history's most powerful personalities and was responsible for starting the Hellenistic Age. The Hellenistic Age was highly significant as it was the platform that spread Ancient Greek culture throughout most of the civilized world.

As mentioned earlier, Alexander was from, and the king of, Macedonia. The Kingdom of Macedonia consisted of Greece, Bulgaria, and all of the former Yugoslavia Republics. In a period of about ten years between the years 334 and 324 B.C.E., Alexander the Great built Macedonia from the ground up and ensured that it was the leading power in the known world.

Alexander the Great conquered an impressive amount of land and in those lands, established a network of military settlements, many of which were to be developed into major cities. The most significant of these cities was known as Alexandria, Egypt, which Alexander the Great founded and named in honor of himself. Alexander the Great had the tendency to name every city after himself, and, in total, there were over 70 cities with the name Alexandria after his conquests. Only Alexandria in Egypt remains, however.

Alexander the Great stabilized the entire Mediterranean economy by establishing a system that utilized coins on a silver standard. This introduction revolutionized trading in the ancient world and strengthened trade throughout his conquered regions. When Alexander circulated a mass amount of silver throughout his conquered lands from the treasures he seized in Persia, the economy strengthened even further. His conquests united the known world, which at the time was made up of three continents—Europe, Africa, and Asia. Through his conquests, he ensured trade was made possible with these lands. Prior to Alexander's Empire, this would never have happened as all the continents were fearful, suspicious, and full of contempt towards one another. Alexander the Great was also responsible for spreading knowledge throughout his Empire. As mentioned earlier Alexander the Great had an inherent fascination with science thanks to his tutor, Aristotle. Alexander spread his knowledge of science, geography, and botany and through his personal interest in these topics, huge advances in these fields were realized.

Because the lands were part of one empire, movement and information were more accessible and less dangerous. He ensured that information could flow freely and regimes that did not permit it were abolished. Thus, knowledge between people and lands was more accessible. He also removed political barriers that prevented individuals from other places from coming into contact with each other. For example, a citizen from Greece could travel freely into Babylonia and vice versa. For the first time, people from different regions and backgrounds were able to see eye to eye, and their different ideas were no longer restricted in the confines of their own nations. Alexander the Great's unified empire was revolutionary as now people were able to make long-distance voyages without having to worry about entering hostile territories of rival countries. Ideas and knowledge were far more accessible, leading to the age of renowned scholars. For example, in the field of mathematics, the revolutionary teachings of Pythagoras and Euclid could spread across borders and educate the civilized world. Alexander the Great was truly an outstanding figure and his influence on the Greek and Ancient world cannot be understated.

CONCLUSION

Ancient Greece and its fascinating mythology is truly a marvel of human history and one that has stood the test of time. The Ancient Greeks practiced a polytheistic belief system that is filled to the brim with captivating tales, myths, gods, goddesses, customs, traditions, and stories that still capture our imagination all these thousands of years later. Throughout our read, we have peeled back the many layers of a complex history that surrounded Ancient Greece and its polytheistic beliefs. In doing so, we have learned a great deal about Ancient Greek culture. We have truly encapsulated what life was like for an Ancient Greek citizens with regards to how their beliefs and numerous gods shaped their society and everything in it. All that we need to know about the Greek pantheon and Ancient Greece has been neatly wrapped into one fascinating read. Throughout our read, we have traveled back in time and peeked through a window to show us what the world was like for the Greeks thousands of years ago.

We covered it all, starting with the creation of the universe, the Titans, the gods, the goddesses, the Cyclopes, and the Hecatonchires. We unpacked how the world began with Chaos, a gaping hole of emptiness, and out of Chaos sprang three more primordial deities. These deities gave birth to many children. These families would go on to have unimaginable conflict leading to terrible tension and horrific actions among one another. A tyrannical rule would come to pass in the form of the Titan Uranus, who would imprison all of his children to ensure they would never overthrow them. Gaee would not stand for such cruelty and freed the youngest Titan child, Cronus, from his father Uranus's grasp. Cronus would go on to slay his father and free his siblings. Cronus had ended the tyrant rule of his father Uranus but history would repeat itself. The Titan Cronus who took over from his father as the ruler of the world was also a tyrant and just like his father, he would imprison his children by devouring them as he feared they would overthrow him. The Titan Cronus would devour five of his six children but fail to devour his sixth child, Zeus, as a result of being tricked by his wife Rhea. Zeus grew into an unimaginably strong god and defeated Cronus while freeing his imprisoned siblings in the process. However, that was not the end of the Titans or Cronus. Zeus and the other Olympian gods fought the Titans for an entire decade. Zeus and the gods of Olympus defeated the Titans and thus Zeus claimed his throne as ruler of the world and shared it with all the other Greek pantheons.

We further unpacked how the Greek pantheon influenced society. Greek mythology led to countless temples built in the god's honors, as well as many festivals being practiced year in and year out. These temples were grand and they were all dedicated to a single god as each god had its own city they would watch over. Greeks from far and wide would bring offerings, gifts, and sacrifices to appease, admire, show respect and gain favor from the gods. Festivals were held on many occasions and there were constantly festivals being held in the name of the gods. There were festivals for all the seasons. Whether it was in summer, spring, autumn, or winter it didn't matter as each season hosted an array of festivals. The festival that is still practiced to this day is the Olympics, but the Olympics of today is far removed from what it was. The Olympics during Ancient Greece were many Greek's favorite festivals filled with athletic games, feasts, and sacrifices in honor of all the gods, but particularly in honor of Zeus. As the Greek world evolved and time began to pass the gods began to be questioned and Greeks started to attempt to debunk the myths, thus the age of the Greek philosophers began. However, despite the attempts of the philosophers trying to propose new explanations about the reality of the world, the majority of the Greek populace still found comfort in their ancient mythological beliefs.

The significance of the gods was evident as seen in all the festivals, sacrifices, and temples built in their honor. It was clear that the Greek pantheon played a significant role in shaping almost every aspect of Ancient Greek society. Thus, it is important that we unpack and highlight the very gods that the Ancient Greeks worshiped and respected so intensely. The Olympian gods were the main gods of Greek mythology. They were made up of 12 gods (six gods and six goddesses) which included Zeus, Hera, Apollo, Hermes, Artemis, Ares, Poseidon, Athena, Demeter, Hestia, Hephaestus, and Aphrodite. They felt human emotions and would often be seen succumbing to them. The Greek pantheon was forever present in the minds of the Ancient Greeks. The Greek pantheon left an enormous legacy behind in human history.

The Olympian gods were not the only significant figures in Greek mythology; there were many minor gods, demigods, mythical creatures, and monsters. Demigods such as Herakles, Achilles, Theseus, Perseus, and Helen of Troy played a significant role in Greek mythology and Ancient Greek society. Minor deities such as the nymphs were also incredibly significant figures and were constantly mentioned throughout the myths of Ancient Greece. Mythical creatures such as centaurs and satyrs also play a part in providing depth to the vast lore of Greek mythology.

What would the Greek myths be without monsters? The monsters were fierce and ferocious and were ever-present in epic battles between them and the Greek pantheon. The monsters of Greek mythology are fascinating and they come in all shapes and sizes. They provide a sense of danger to the myths and forever capture our imagination with their descriptions, powers, and presence. There are thousands of monsters in Greek mythology, although we only unpacked four of the most legendary monsters in all of Greek mythology— Medusa, the Hydra, Typhon, and Cerberus. Throughout our read, we were exposed to many myths and legends. Some of the most interesting myths include the myth of Icarus, Pandora's box, the abduction of Persephone, and the love story of Eros and Psyche. Throughout our read, we have covered so many myths that it is hard to simply pick which are the best ones as each myth is as exciting, if not more exciting, than the last.

In Greek mythology, many battles were fought, but few can argue any battle more significant, famous, and legendary than the epic Trojan War. We unpacked how the conflict began and what the catalyst for the war between the Greeks and the Trojans truly was. Turned out it was a golden apple and three vanity-fueled goddesses. However, the Trojan War was truly an epic battle and is a story that will be told until the end of time. Other battles that were truly influential included the many conquests of Alexander the Great. Alexander the Great was one of, if not the most, influential figures in human history, and his influence over Greece and the Ancient world was revolutionary.

Greek mythology is fascinating and it is no surprise that the ancient myths from thousands of years ago are still being studied and told today. These myths might be thousands of years old, but they still have great relevance today. These myths were not just stories, they were lessons and held many secrets regarding how the Ancient Greeks lived their lives. If there is one thing we can take away from our read through it is the immense influence the Greek pantheon played in Ancient Greek society and how the Greeks were inherently influenced by the epic tales and myths that surrounded this fascinating polytheistic belief system. The Greek pantheon may not be worshipped anymore but their legacy will live on forever and have a stained history for hundreds of years to come.

REFERENCES

Adkins, A. W. H., & Richard, J. (2018). Greek mythology | Gods, Stories, & History. In *Encyclopædia Britannica*. https://www.britannica.com/topic/Greek-mythology

Ancient Greek Mythology. (2015). *Sacred places*. Ancient Greek Mythology. https://welcometothegreekreligion.weebly.com/sacred-places.html#:~:text=The%20Parthenon%20on%20the%20Acropolis%20in%20Ancient%20Athens%2C

Ancient Literature. (2020, November 6). *Artemis' Personality, Character Traits, Strengths and Weaknesses*. Ancient Literature. https://www.ancient-literature.com/artemis-personality/

Baring the Aegis. (2020). *The festivals of early Boedromion*. The Festivals of Early Boedromion. https://baringtheaegis.blogspot.com/2013/09/the-festivals-of-early-boedromion.html

Britannica. (2018a). Hermes | Greek mythology. In *Encyclopædia Britannica*. https://www.britannica.com/topic/Hermes-Greek-mythology

Britannica. (2018b). Aphrodite | Mythology, Worship, & Art. In *Encyclopædia Britannica*. https://www.britannica.com/topic/Aphrodite-Greek-mythology

Britannica. (2018c). Ares | God, Myths, Siblings, & Family. In *Encyclopædia Britannica*. https://www.britannica.com/topic/Ares-Greek-mythology

Britannica. (2018d). Apollo | Facts, Symbols, & Myths. In *Encyclopædia Britannica*.

https://www.britannica.com/topic/Apollo-Greek-mythology

Britannica. (2018e). Zeus | Myths, Wife, Children, & Facts. In *Encyclopædia Britannica*. https://www.britannica.com/topic/Zeus

Britannica. (2019a). Panathenaea | Greek festival | Britannica. In *Encyclopædia Britannica*. https://www.britannica.com/topic/Panathenaea

Britannica. (2019b). Artemis | Myths, Symbols, & Meaning. In *Encyclopædia Britannica*. https://www.britannica.com/topic/Artemis-Greek-goddess

Britannica. (2020). Nymph | Greek mythology | Britannica. In *Encyclopædia Britannica*. https://www.britannica.com/topic/nymph-Greek-mythology

Campbell, M. (2007, February 12). *Meaning, origin and history of the name Poseidon*. Behind the Name. https://www.behindthename.com/name/poseidon

Cartwright, M. (2012, July 29). *Greek Mythology*. Ancient History Encyclopedia; Ancient History Encyclopedia. https://www.ancient.eu/Greek_Mythology/

Cartwright, M. (2018). *Trojan War*. World History Encyclopedia. https://www.worldhistory.org/Trojan_War/

Davis, E. (2018). *characteristics and symbols*. Athena. https://elissadavis.weebly.com/characteristics-and-symbols.html

Decibelboy. (2012, November 16). *Mythology, does it explore or hide?* Decibelboy. https://decibelboy.wordpress.com/mythology-does-it-explore-or-hide/

Dilouambaka, E. (2014). *A Brief History Of The Temple Of Poseidon, Sounion*. Culture Trip. https://theculturetrip.com/europe/greece/athens/articles/a-brief-history-of-the-temple-of-poseidon-sounion/

Encyclopedia.com. (2019). *Satyr | Encyclopedia.com*. Www.encyclopedia.com.

https://www.encyclopedia.com/literature-and-arts/classical-literature-mythology-and-folklore/folklore-and-mythology/satyr

Gill, N. S. (2003a, October 8). *What You Need to Know About the Greek God Zeus*. ThoughtCo; ThoughtCo. https://www.thoughtco.com/profile-of-the-greek-god-zeus-111915

Gill, N. S. (2003b, October 17). *Hermes Greek God*. ThoughtCo; ThoughtCo. https://www.thoughtco.com/hermes-greek-god-111910

Gill, N. S. (2019a). *Greek Winter Solstice Celebrations in Honor of Poseidon*. ThoughtCo. https://www.thoughtco.com/greek-winter-solstice-celebrations-120989

Gill, N. S. (2019b). *Pregnant King Carries Baby in His Head: The Birth of Athena*. ThoughtCo. https://www.thoughtco.com/athena-the-greek-goddess-of-wisdom-111905

Goddess Guide. (2008). *Athena The Greek Goddess*. Goddess-Guide.com. https://www.goddess-guide.com/athena.html

Greek Boston. (2016, November 22). *Children of Zeus and Hera in Greek Mythology*. Greekboston.com. https://www.greekboston.com/culture/mythology/children-zeus-hera/

Greek Gods and Goddesses. (2014, September 19). *Poseidon • Facts and Information on Greek God Poseidon*. Greek Gods & Goddesses. https://greekgodsandgoddesses.net/gods/poseidon/

Greek Gods and Goddesses. (2016). *Centaurs • Facts and Information about the Greek Mythological Creature*. Greek Gods & Goddesses. https://greekgodsandgoddesses.net/myths/centaurs/

Greek Gods and Goddesses. (2017). *Hera • Facts and Information on Greek Goddess Hera*. Greek Gods & Goddesses. https://greekgodsandgoddesses.net/goddesses/hera

/#:~:text=Hera%20is%20the%20Queen%20of%20the%20Gods%20and

Greek Gods and Goddesses. (2017). *Typhon - The Father of All Monsters | Greek Myths and Monsters*. Greek Gods & Goddesses. https://greekgodsandgoddesses.net/gods/typhon/

Greek Mythology. (2017). *Poseidon :: Greek God of the Sea*. Www.greekmythology.com. https://www.greekmythology.com/Olympians/Poseidon/poseidon.html#:~:text=Poseidon%20is%20the%20violent%20and%20ill-tempered%20god%20of

Greek Travelers. (2019, December 19). *30 of the Most Famous Tales from Greek Mythology*. Greektraveltellers.com. https://greektraveltellers.com/blog/30-of-the-most-famous-tales-from-greek-mythology

Greekgod.info. (2019). *Greek god Zeus, the King of the Gods and Ruler of Mankind*. Greek-Gods.info. https://www.greek-gods.info/greek-gods/zeus/

Greekgods.info. (2019). *Greek God Hermes, the God of the Trade and Messenger of the Gods*. Www.greek-Gods.info. https://www.greek-gods.info/greek-gods/hermes/#:~:text=Appearance%20of%20Hermes%20Hermes%20was%20depicted%20as%20a

GreekMythology.com. (2017, May 26). *The Creation II - Greek Mythology*. Greekmythology.com; GreekMythology.com. https://www.greekmythology.com/Myths/The_Myths/The_Creation_II/the_creation_ii.html

GreekMythology.com. (2018a, March 13). *Hera - Greek Mythology*. Greekmythology.com; GreekMythology.com. https://www.greekmythology.com/Olympians/Hera/hera.html

GreekMythology.com. (2018b, March 13). *Theseus - Greek Mythology*. Greekmythology.com; GreekMythology.com. https://www.greekmythology.com/Myths/Heroes/Theseus/theseus.html

GreekMythology.com. (2018c, May 20). *The Creation - Greek Mythology*. Greekmythology.com; GreekMythology.com. https://www.greekmythology.com/Myths/The_Myths/The_Creation/the_creation.html

GreekMythology.com. (2018d, November 14). *Eros and Psyche - Greek Mythology*. Greekmythology.com; GreekMythology.com. https://www.greekmythology.com/Myths/The_Myths/Eros_and_Psyche/eros_and_psyche.html

Hellenion. (2021). *Skiraphoria / Skira – Hellenion*. Skiraphoria. https://www.hellenion.org/festivals/skiraphoria/

Hellenismos and Me. (2019). *Mounukhion*. Hellenismos and Me. https://hellenismosandme.tumblr.com/post/48532766292/mounukhion

Hill, B. (2015, May 30). *Cerberus: Legendary Hell Hound of the Underworld*. Ancient Origins; Ancient Origins. https://www.ancient-origins.net/myths-legends-europe/cerberus-legendary-hell-hound-underworld-003142

International Olympic Committee. (2021, April 27). *Welcome to the Ancient Olympic Games*. International Olympic Committee. https://olympics.com/ioc/ancient-olympic-games

Ivy Panda. (2019). *Political and cultural impact of Alexander the Great's conquests - 1355 Words | Essay Example*. Ivypanda.com. https://ivypanda.com/essays/political-and-cultural-impact-of-alexander-the-greats-conquests/

Legends and Chronicles. (2019). *Hydra | Mythological Greek Hydra | Greek Hydra Mythology*. Legendsandchronicles.com. http://www.legendsandchronicles.com/mythological-greek-creatures/hydra/

Lloyd, J. (2015). *The Anthesteria*. World History Encyclopedia. https://www.worldhistory.org/The_Anthesteria/

M. A., L., & B. A., L. (2016). *How Did the Norse Believe the World Was Created?* Learn Religions. https://www.learnreligions.com/creation-in-norse-mythology-117868

Nangia, N. (2020). *The Original Story Of Pandora's Box.* Onehowto.com. https://education.onehowto.com/article/the-original-story-of-pandora-s-box-12643.html

Need for Science. (2020, September 7). *Alexander the Great: Life and Conquests | Need For Science.* Alexander the Great: Life and Conquests. https://www.needforscience.com/history/alexander-the-great-life-and-conquests/

Opsopaus, J. (1996). *Ancient Greek Samhain Festivals.* Opsopaus.com. http://opsopaus.com/OM/BA/GSF.html

Pagan Paths. (2020). *Greek paganism (Greco pagan).* Pagans and Wiccans Welcome. https://paganpaths.weebly.com/greek-paganism-greco-pagan.html

Reference.com. (2020). *What Is a Physical Description of Aphrodite?* Reference. https://www.reference.com/world-view/physical-description-aphrodite-271879e15f37534e

Singing for Her. (2016, May 27). *Plunteria.* Singing for Her. https://singingforher.wordpress.com/2016/05/27/plunteria/

Smith, G. (2020). *Why Ancient Greek Mythology is Still Relevant Today.* Corespirit.com. https://corespirit.com/articles/why-ancient-greek-mythology-is-still-relevant-today

Tales Beyond Belief. (2017a). *Demigods* ***. Talesbeyondbelief.com. http://www.talesbeyondbelief.com/greek-gods-mythology/demigods.htm

Tales Beyond Belief. (2017b). *Temple of Zeus* ***. Www.talesbeyondbelief.com.

http://www.talesbeyondbelief.com/greek-gods-mythology/temple-of-zeus.htm

The Brittish Museum. (2019). *Ancient Greece - Festivals and Games - The British Museum*. Ancientgreece.co.uk. http://www.ancientgreece.co.uk/festivals/home_set.html

The trials of Apollo. (2018). *Zeus*. Riordan Wiki. https://riordan.fandom.com/wiki/Zeus#:~:text=Zeus%20is%20very%20tall%2C%20imposing%2C%20and%20very%20muscular%2C

Theoi. (2020). *Nymphs | Theoi Greek Mythology*. Www.theoi.com. https://www.theoi.com/greek-mythology/nymphs.html

Thought Co. (2019). *Greatest and Mightiest Heroes of Greek Mythology*. ThoughtCo. https://www.thoughtco.com/greatest-greek-heroes-118992

Violatti, C. (2014, May 27). *Ionia*. Ancient History Encyclopedia; Ancient History Encyclopedia. https://www.ancient.eu/ionia/

Wikipedia. (2018, December 3). *Apollo*. Wikipedia; Wikimedia Foundation. https://en.wikipedia.org/wiki/Apollo

OTHER BOOKS BY HISTORY BROUGHT ALIVE

- Ancient Egypt: Discover Fascinating History, Mythology, Gods, Goddesses, Pharaohs, Pyramids, and More from the Mysterious Ancient Egyptian Civilization.

Available now on Kindle, Paperback, Hardcover & Audio in all regions

- Greek Mythology: Explore The Timeless Tales Of Ancient Greece, The Myths, History & Legends of The Gods, Goddesses, Titans, Heroes, Monsters & More

Available now on Kindle, Paperback, Hardcover & Audio in all regions

- Mythology for Kids: Explore Timeless Tales, Characters, History, & Legendary Stories from Around the World. Norse, Celtic, Roman, Greek, Egypt & Many More

Available now on Kindle, Paperback, Hardcover & Audio in all regions

- Mythology of Mesopotamia: Fascinating

Insights, Myths, Stories & History From The World's Most Ancient Civilization. Sumerian, Akkadian, Babylonian, Persian, Assyrian and More

Available now on Kindle, Paperback, Hardcover & Audio in all regions

- Norse Magic & Runes: A Guide To The Magic, Rituals, Spells & Meanings of Norse Magick, Mythology & Reading The Elder Futhark Runes

Available now on Kindle, Paperback, Hardcover & Audio in all regions

- Norse Mythology, Vikings, Magic & Runes: Stories, Legends & Timeless Tales From Norse & Viking Folklore + A Guide To The Rituals, Spells & Meanings of Norse Magick & The Elder Futhark Runes. (3 books in 1)

Available now on Kindle, Paperback, Hardcover & Audio in all regions

- Norse Mythology: Captivating Stories & Timeless Tales Of Norse Folklore. The Myths, Sagas & Legends of The Gods, Immortals, Magical Creatures, Vikings & More

Available now on Kindle, Paperback, Hardcover & Audio in all regions

- Norse Mythology for Kids: Legendary Stories, Quests & Timeless Tales from Norse Folklore. The Myths, Sagas & Epics of the Gods, Immortals, Magic Creatures, Vikings & More

Available now on Kindle, Paperback, Hardcover & Audio in all regions

- Roman Empire: Rise & The Fall. Explore The History, Mythology, Legends, Epic Battles & Lives Of The Emperors, Legions, Heroes, Gladiators & More

Available now on Kindle, Paperback, Hardcover & Audio in all regions

- The Vikings: Who Were The Vikings? Enter The Viking Age & Discover The Facts, Sagas, Norse Mythology, Legends, Battles & More

Available now on Kindle, Paperback, Hardcover & Audio in all regions

FREE BONUS FROM HBA: EBOOK BUNDLE

Greetings!

First of all, thank you for reading our books. As fellow passionate readers of History and Mythology, we aim to create the very best books for our readers.

Now, we invite you to join our VIP list. As a welcome gift, we offer the History & Mythology Ebook Bundle below for free. Plus, you can be the first to receive new books and exclusives! Remember it's 100% free to join.

Simply scan the QR code to join.

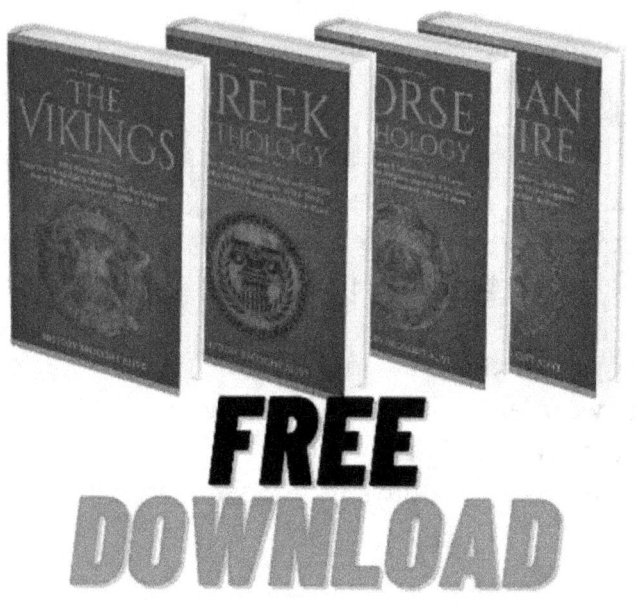

https://www.subscribepage.com/hba

Keep up to date with us on:
YouTube: History Brought Alive
Facebook: History Brought Alive
www.historybroughtalive.com

www.ingramcontent.com/pod-product-compliance
Lightning Source LLC
Chambersburg PA
CBHW070106120526
44588CB00032B/1162